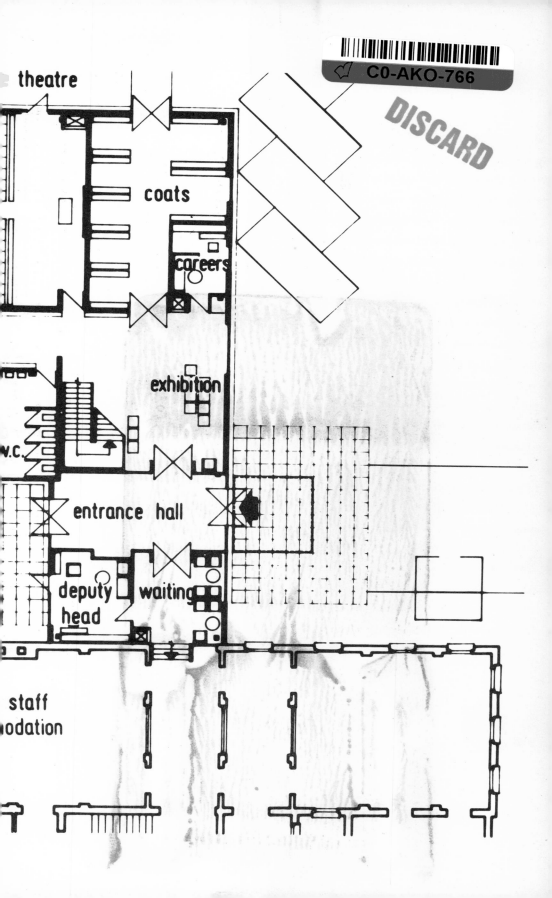

theatre

coats

careers

exhibition

w.c.

entrance hall

deputy head

waiting

staff
odation

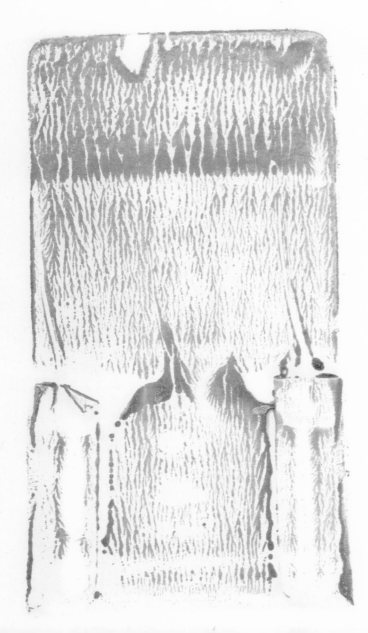

COMMUNICATION
AND LEARNING

COMMUNICATION AND LEARNING

LEN S. POWELL

AMERICAN ELSEVIER PUBLISHING COMPANY, INC.
New York   1969

American Edition Published by
American Elsevier Publishing Company, Inc.
52 Vanderbilt Avenue, New York, New York 10017

Standard Book Number 444–19745–1
Library of Congress Catalog Card Number: 79–82742

Printed in Great Britain

To my wife

PREFACE

This book is about teaching, instructing, training, explaining, persuading; about the whole repertoire of activities we go through in order to get people to learn. It is written for the doers who make the tactical decisions, who learn the footwork, who know at first hand the real achievements and the real disasters. There are the thinkers who think strategies and there are the technologists who invent machines to teach with but in the end, when all the thinking has been thought and all the equipment has been made it is we who stand in the classroom and answer for what goes on.

So it starts by looking at the process of communication from the learner's point of view—at learning theory and perception—and goes on to discuss the effect of group size and then examines the variety of equipment at our disposal and the ways in which it can help us. It finishes, rather obviously, by saying that since the object of the performance is to make learning as efficient as possible, then for Heaven's sake let the arena be a suitable one.

L.S.P.

ACKNOWLEDGEMENTS

I don't want to blame anyone else for this book but to thank those who have done their best with me in the course of my writing it. And so I am sincerely grateful to Jean Lovell, David Reeder and Bill Stephen who read chapters and made valuable comments on them and to Ann Dryland who read the whole manuscript and helped me enormously. I am grateful too, to Peter Perry, the Director of BACIE, for allowing me to use again what I had written for his publications. Then there is Alain Davey who made the drawings, Doreen Heatley who did much more than turn some shocking scribble into comprehensible typescript, and my daughter Jane who came to the rescue whenever I decided to write something else instead. Perhaps, on second thoughts, she should take the blame.

CONTENTS

The Plates are positioned at the end of the book.

THE PROCESS IN THEORY

1 LEARNING

The word communication, like most words in a living language, can be moulded into the cast of its context. Here we shall limit its meaning to the process by which one person is made aware of ideas in the mind of another and we shall examine only those facets of the process that seem relevant to the promotion of learning.

Learning goes beyond the mere awareness of sensory impressions to the acquisition of skills and knowledge, to the development of attitudes, beliefs and standards. And since what is learned can be apparent only through expression of some kind or another, learning is observable through changes in a person's responses to impressions.

We shall further limit our examination to those forms of communication which are quite deliberately directed towards training or teaching and ignore the complex of transient impressions which, despite their total power to persuade and inform, derive from sources and motives which are not primarily pedagogical.

Many of the concepts to which we shall refer need constant reappraisal and many of the value judgements call for analysis, but these too are outside the scope of the present discussion.

There are some people who appear to have an instinctive awareness of the most direct and effective way of communicating. These include the great music-hall artists, great orators and great conversationalists: men and women who, without detailed study, are able to get in touch and keep in touch with the intellects and emotions of other people: there are born teachers. But most of us acquire a degree of facility in the art of communicating by study, by discovering what appears to happen when learning occurs, by analysing the influence of intelligence on the preferred mode of communication or the mode on the memory and so on, but first of all through study. And then as we prepare lessons or speeches or broadcasts we consciously construct our presentation against a background of theory, knowing that the reassurance which comes from our foresight enhances our power and confidence. And it is thus that we haul ourselves above mediocrity.

Leaving aside detailed analysis, there are a number of broad requirements that must be satisfied before learning can be efficient. For example, the learner must be *able* to learn what the teacher sets out to teach. This, in turn, depends upon his physical well-being, his intellectual capacity and his current knowledge and skill. The learner must also be willing to co-operate—he must *want* to learn. This may result from one or more pressures—the need for a more secure job, the fear of the consequences of failure or the fun of the study itself and so on, but unless the learner wants to learn—unless he is motivated—he will not do so.

There are also certain strategies that must be adopted if the effort which he puts into learning is to be minimized, certain sequences of study, certain procedures, certain breaks and so on. In formal education the basic plans for teaching and learning are framed on the one hand by such limits as terms, lengths of periods, the provision for homework and holidays, and on the other hand by syllabuses and examinations. The detailed strategy of day-to-day learning is left to teachers in planning their lessons and adapting them as they teach. It is within this framework that the teaching-learning in formal education occurs.

Training officers must also fit their work into a defined framework and, indeed, may be required to decide upon some of its dimensions themselves. They too will have scope for manoeuvre within the training periods even though their programmes may of necessity be more rigorously delineated.

THE MECHANICS OF LEARNING

Our macroscopic observations—that people learn when they are able to do so and when they want to do so, can be props for the organization of effective communication: that learning sometimes seems to be dominated by the process of conditioning, sometimes by the structuring of insights and sometimes by the learner's struggle to prove himself, can, with profit, prescribe the most promising method. But both for our professional satisfaction and for tactical resilience we should get and keep in touch with the science of human behaviour. The following paragraphs are intended to direct attention to this area of study.

The first important researches into this field were carried out by Professor E. L. Thorndike of Columbia University in New York and published by him in 1911.[1] Typical of his experiments was a series in which a hungry cat had to get out of a maze in order to find food. At first the cat behaved in an erratic and excited fashion but was ultimately successful. Repeated trials reduced the number of errors until the cat "learned" the route to the food. Experiments of this kind suggested that the basis of this learning is trial and error which leads to ultimate satisfaction through success.

In one of another group of experiments, Thorndike put a hungry cat into a cage through the bars of which it could see and smell food. Inside the cage was a lever which, when it was pressed, would release the cat and enable it to get food.

At first the cat struggled frantically to get out by pushing, scratching, squeezing and pawing until, by chance, it operated the lever. As further trials were made, the cat operated the lever with fewer useless preliminaries until ultimately it did so immediately upon being shut into the cage. This process of trial-and-error learning which has been formulated in detail by B. F. Skinner is called by him operant conditioning: conditioning which results from the subject operating on its environment.

Thorndike concluded that all learning was the result of the reward which came from success after trial-and-error behaviour. Although, from the point of view of research, his conclusions have been superseded, learning does occur in the kinds of circumstances which he cites and if human subjects are provided with similar experiences they too will learn: if these experiences provide a more efficient route to learning than others there may be value in exploiting them. Furthermore, an extension of the work initiated by Thorndike has led to one kind of programmed learning the value of which is abundantly evident as we shall see in Chapter 9.

Critics of Thorndike's trial-and-error theory based their views on the objection that his experiments were so designed as to give the solutions they did, that cats, for example, cannot learn all they learn through solving problems of this kind to these ends. They maintained that the tension set up by an obstruction between the subject and the desired goal gives rise, not to a single force, but to a complex of forces which, at the moment of solution are *suddenly* reorganized to produce satisfaction through success: this is an important component of Gestalt theory. They held that the whole is more than the parts and that the significance of a situation or pattern of stimuli is revealed by its total pattern and not in the separate elements of which it is composed.

The views of the Gestalt psychologists were supported by the experiments of Köhler in Germany in the 1920s in which he investigated the problem-solving abilities of chimpanzees. In one such group of experiments he showed that, having learned to pull a banana into its cage with a short stick, a chimpanzee could solve the following problem. Inside its cage was a short stick A and outside it a banana which was beyond reach with this stick (*Fig. 1*). At the other end of the cage and just outside it was a long stick B. The ape first tried to reach the fruit with the short stick, failed and became angry and frustrated. It then wandered around looking at the sticks and the banana until, quite suddenly, it picked up the short stick, pulled in the long one and then used it to reach the banana. This, said Köhler, was the result of insight, of seeing the whole situation, of picking out the essential components which must fit the situation and then fitting them together in the mind. This sudden awareness of a "way out" is a common experience in human learning and knowing about it can be exploited to the end of efficient teaching.

The basic objection to the "insight" explanation is that it is simply a verbal cloak for a process which must occur beneath it. Recent experiments[2]

3

show that this sudden synthesis may just as suddenly lead to a wrong solution which, in the absence of criteria for assessing it, will be reached again and again if the same subject is presented with the same problem in the same circumstances. Further, the synthesis is always preceded by experience or

FIG. 1. The situation in one of Köhler's experiments

training in the separate components from which the solution is integrated and this points to learning being a more or less complex construct of conditioned responses. This, however, does not detract from the validity of exploiting the observable gross strategies which lead to successful learning through the apparent structuring of insights.

CONDITIONING

The process of learning to recognize, associate and discriminate as a consequence of "operating" on the environment, of rejecting what does not reduce discomfort and repeating what brings satisfaction, is regarded as the basic building process of learning. This is not surprising if we think in terms of evolution. An amoeba consists of a single cell which performs all of the functions necessary to maintain itself and propagate its species. Its behaviour is therefore controlled by forces which cause it to encompass food by the most direct means available to it, to discriminate between what it can digest and what it cannot and to reproduce itself when it has sufficient "life" to become two separate cells. It would be silly to suggest that one amoeba could be more intelligent than another but it is certainly true that their rate of activity is a direct function of their environment.

In creatures of a higher order, groups of cells have separate functions and hence the onset of hunger, for example, will set up a number of interconnected responses all of which are designed to reduce the discomfort with the minimum expenditure of energy in the shortest possible time. This may involve a series of manoeuvres which, for maximum efficiency, must be performed in a particular sequence. This more complex pattern of response is not entirely automatic (reflex) since it needs to be different in different circumstances. The process of selection by which these patterns are established is learning.

A human being is a complex of cells which, by adapting themselves to their physical and chemical environments, maintain equilibrium. Some adaptations are very simple. If, for example, groups of cells are compressed they change their relative positions and shapes so as to reduce the damaging effect of the pressure—all substances do this to a greater or less degree. But other adaptations are very complicated and involve servo-responses of great delicacy. These are the adaptations which ensure the survival of the individual or his species and which, for convenience, are said to be regulated by drives,[3] one of which is, of course, hunger.

Each drive is controlled by a group of cells and these groups, or centres, form a cluster in a small area called the hypothalamus at the base of the brain in the middle of the head (Fig. 2). As with normal servomechanisms, each drive is under the control of two centres working in opposition to each other: one of them switches the drive on and the other extinguishes it. The hunger centres, for example, are activated by the concentration of blood sugar.[4] When the amount of sugar falls below a certain level one group of the so-called glucoreceptors switch on the drive and the brain registers hunger. When food is eaten, the level of sugar rises very quickly and the inhibitory glucoreceptor is excited and extinguishes the hunger. This explains why we recover from the sensation of hunger soon after the commencement of a meal and not, as we might expect, after the digestive process has had time to be effective. This theory is supported by experiments of the kind in which electrodes implanted in the brain of a live rat and joined by flexible leads to a

5

battery can be made to take over the switching process. When the drive centre is switched on the rat is hungry and will seek and eat food: when it is switched off the animal—even though physically in need of food—will exhibit no interest in finding it.

Other similar experiments also lead to the conclusion that animal behaviour is regulated by these "on-off" controls which are situated in the central nervous system and that, with repetition, the control mechanisms reproduce

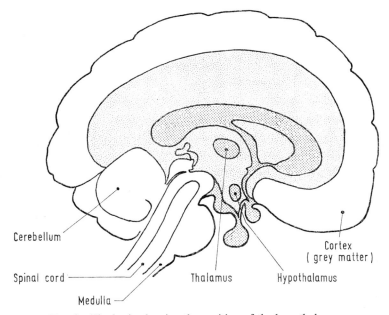

FIG. 2. The brain showing the position of the hypothalamus

ever more automatically responses which result in the extinction of drives and gradually eradicate those responses which prove ineffectual.

In human beings the process is complicated by the fact that we are able to internalize our experiences in the form of language and, as a consequence, to control most of our bodily functions in a fashion which is called voluntary. Now at root, these "voluntary" decisions can be regarded as a complex of adjustments of cells, none of which is any more voluntary than the movement of an amoeba enveloping its food. If this is taken as the starting point, learning is the *involuntary* adaptation of responses to environmental pressures and, the limit of the complexity of learning of which any individual is capable is set by the physico-chemical characteristics of his organism. This kind of thinking lies behind the behaviourist theories of learning and experiments with programmed instruction show that deliberately providing for this process can promote very efficient learning.

6

TEACHING BY CONDITIONING

Immediate evidence of the exploitation of conditioning may be observed during the training of animals: it seems to follow one of two patterns. The first, which was investigated and reported by Pavlov at the beginning of this century, is called classical or Pavlovian conditioning. This consists of replacing a "natural" or unconditional stimulus by a contrived one in such a

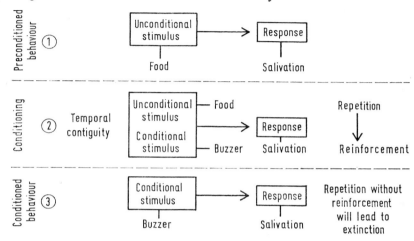

FIG. 3. The sequence of classical conditioning

way that the response normally associated with the former is elicited by the latter (*Fig. 3*).

Typical of Pavlov's experiments was one in which he pressed a buzzer at the same time as he offered food to a dog. The dog's unconditional response to seeing and smelling the food was to salivate and after the process had been repeated a number of times the dog salivated on hearing the buzzer even when no food was near. The repetition of the buzzer–food link (the conditional stimulus and the unconditional stimulus in temporal contiguity) makes the conditioning stronger and is therefore said to reinforce the response. If, however, the buzzer is repeatedly pressed and no food given the tie between the buzzer and salivation weakens until the conditional stimulus is no longer followed by the response—the conditioning is extinguished.

This substitution of an existing stimulus by a contrived one is the simplest form of learning and is well known to anyone who keeps animals of any kind. From it more complex constructs may be developed as, for example, in training a dog to shut a door at the words of command. The sequence is as follows:

1. Starve the dog for about a day.
2. Hold the dog in the centre of a room whilst an assistant holds a small

7

    piece of meat against an open door and slightly above the normal stretch of the dog's head.

3. Give the command and release the dog at the same time. It will run to the food, jump against the door in order to reach and, as it eats the food, its paws will close the door.
4. Pat the dog and praise it.

Repeat this sequence making the same command each time until the dog will obey without getting any meat from the assistant's hand and continue beyond this stage until it is no longer necessary for a hand to be held against the door.

The response which the dog now seeks is no longer the food since it is no longer hungry, but the praise. The command—a conditional stimulus—now causes the dog to shut the door—a conditional response—in order to earn praise—the reinforcement. So long as the same command is given and the dog is praised for responding correctly it will always shut the door when it is told to do so. With a little extra training it can be taught to shut any door.

In the cat and maze example given earlier, the animal had to respond correctly *before* it could find satisfaction and this process is called operant conditioning. The best known work in this area was done by Professor B. F. Skinner[5,6] of which the following experiment is typical. A hungry pigeon was kept in a cage fitted with a food chute. A disc was fitted on to one side of the cage and when the bird pecked it a pellet of food dropped down the chute. At first the bird pecked at random until, by chance, it triggered off the release and received food. Next time it achieved success more quickly and so on until ultimately it fed by pecking the disc and then the released pellets in rapid succession.

In human affairs, learning by conditioning is frequently exploited. One masterly exponent of the art is the drill sergeant who uses the process to train his men to obey commands. When he wants them to stand to attention, for example, he shouts out a noise which, being interpreted, means, "You must now stand to attention." The noise he makes is quite unique and has a timbre and rhythm which evoke a sense of urgency: it never varies. This is the stimulus to which he wants his men to respond immediately and without conscious thought. When first he makes the noise at them he takes up the posture he wants them to assume and this they attempt to copy. If they do precisely what he has in mind he keeps quiet: this silence is a reward. If, on the other hand, one of them does not take up the required posture he marches briskly across to him and explains sharply how he expects his order to be obeyed. Avoiding this "explaining sharply" is negative reinforcement. After a short time repetition of the stimulus will produce the required response under almost any conceivable conditions.

Some of the characteristics of learning by conditioning may be observed in the following experiment. The learner is told to try to remember eight numbers which will first be read to him twice. He is also told that after he says each number, the correct one will be told to him, whether he is right or wrong, and if he cannot remember a particular number he should say any one that comes into his head. He should count off the eight tries with his fingers and, in all, he may have about thirty attempts to repeat the set correctly.

The numbers are then read out to the learner taking about a quarter of a minute for each set of eight and then the learner is asked to repeat them. As he does so his correct attempts are denoted by a cross on a prepared chart

Attempt	34	19	28	52	71	85	53	92
1	✕	✕						✕
2	✕	✕						✕
3	✕	✕	✕				✕	✕
4	✕	✕	✕				✕	✕
5	✕	✕	✕				✕	✕
6	✕	✕	✕	✕			✕	✕
7	✕	✕	✕	✕			✕	✕
8	✕	✕	✕	✕			✕	✕
9	✕	✕	✕	✕			✕	✕
10	✕	✕	✕	✕	✕		✕	✕
11	✕	✕	✕	✕	✕	✕	✕	✕

FIG. 4. Sequence of learning by operant conditioning

(which he cannot see) and it will be found that, in general, there is a tendency for the learning to follow the pattern shown in *Fig. 4*.

The first attempts may not fit the pattern at all, depending on the learner's short-term memory, sense of apprehension and so on, but usually the first two or three numbers and the last one will be remembered and reinforced almost from the beginning. The remainder will be learned more slowly and generally each additional piece of learning will be an extension of what is already known. Naturally there can be wide variations due to association with numbers which have some significance for the learner and to other factors.

From this kind of experiment we see that learning in this way will be most effective if the amount of material is just small enough for the learner to be right the first time he tries to remember it. Then repetition leads to immediate reinforcement.

9

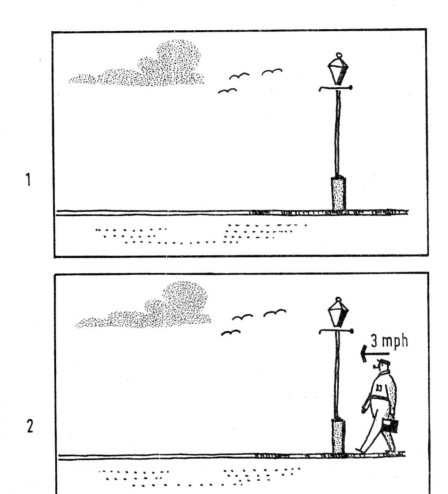

FIG. 5. Set of overhead projector transparencies for teaching the principle of relative velocity

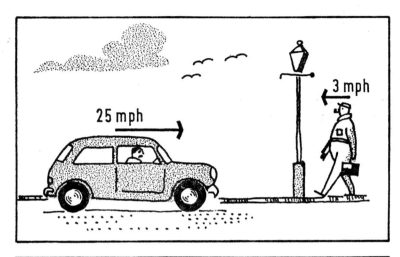

FIG. 5 (cont.)

Notice that in this experiment there is no "sense" in what is learned and that the first and last impressions make a greater impact than the rest. If the experiment is continued for some twenty times after the learner is successful he will find it difficult to forget the numbers.

In classroom teaching the conditioning may be subtle or obvious. An example of the former may occur during a foreign language discussion with a student who is just mastering a particular pronunciation difficulty. Each time the student is correct the teacher immediately makes a slight nod of assent and shows pleasure: each time he is wrong the teacher immediately corrects the error. (This technique has been used by *students* to increase the frequency with which a *lecturer* scratched his head!)

The following example in which the process is obvious involves the use of overlays projected from an overhead projector and introduces the concept of relative velocity (*Fig. 5*).

T   How fast is the lamp-post moving along the street . . . Smith?

S   It isn't moving at all.

T   Good. Now can anyone give the same answer but using the word velocity?

S   Its velocity is zero.

T   Fine. Its velocity relative to the street is zero. What is the velocity of the street relative to the lamp-post?

S   That is zero, too.

T   Good. Now tell me the velocity of the man relative to the lamp-post.

S   Three miles an hour.

.
.
.
.
.
.

T   See if you can explain in a sentence, such as I have been using, the way the dog and the car are moving one to the other.

S   The dog is moving with a velocity of seventeen miles an hour relative to the car.

When similar words, facts or concepts are learnt together, confusion can arise and the teacher should emphasize differences to help discrimination. Equally, drawing attention to similarities aids generalization and this, in turn, can lead to transfer of learning. If, for example, the stimulus is gradually changed and the response to it kept the same, learning of the first stimulus-response association will transfer positively to the new one. If on the other

12

hand the stimulus is kept constant and the response suddenly altered, the learning of the first association interferes with the learning of the second. This is negative transfer. This occurs when, for example, identical pieces of equipment are used for the teaching of two different concepts as when the slide-wire bridge is on one occasion a Wheatstone's bridge for copmaring

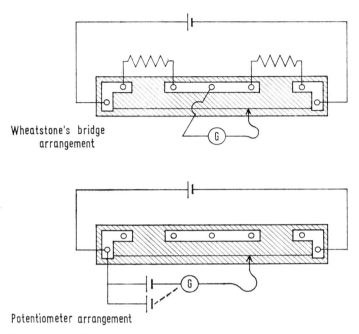

Wheatstone's bridge
arrangement

Potentiometer arrangement

FIG. 6. Two different concepts to be learned from the same equipment

resistances and shortly afterwards is a potentiometer for comparing electromotive forces (*Fig.* 6).

Positive transfer leads to a general method of solving groups of problems with common characteristics and the procedure we follow as a result of this is called a learning set. Because a set develops from and leads to success on many specific occasions it is, by its nature, strongly reinforced and consequently persists for a long time as a source of further understanding.

Learning then, is the development of more and more adaptations to environment by the internalization of experiences and their organization into so-called schemata. Schematic behaviour results from the integration of specific responses into a complex activity and this is capable of wide application and development.

Arbitrary links of stimulus to response such as occur in rote learning do not lead to the development of schemata or to learning of concepts. Without stimulus generalization there can be no transfer of learning and consequently rote learning tends to be inefficient.

Learning progresses therefore as a result of the development of factual connexions into complexes which, in turn become linked by common abstract qualities into concepts. This growth depends to a considerable degree upon linguistic ability which, in turn, derives in a large measure from the richness and balance of the learner's cultural background.

In this way the students learn the facts from which the concept of relative velocities will be structured by finding satisfying responses to the stimuli to which they are exposed.

UNWITTING LEARNING

Most of what we learn unwittingly can be explained in terms of conditioning. The following incident is typical of this process.

In 1961, a London electrical engineering firm began taking parties of students around its departments at fairly regular intervals. When each party reached the model shop they were always halted near to a particular machine which was used by a craftsman who took very little interest in what he did although he was highly skilled. The work the students saw on the machine always attracted their interest and admiration and they tended to linger over it and to ask questions, and after a time it was noticeable that this had had an effect upon the craftsman. His bench and machine became perfectly tidy and orderly and not only did he answer questions which were asked him but he developed an almost professional capacity for making lucid explanations.

The power of reinforcement may equally lead to unexpected failures. For example, a little girl of the writer's acquaintance persisted in moving herself across the floor on her bottom long after reaching the age when she was ready to walk: indeed she even developed a shape suited to this performance. Her mode of locomotion was amusing: she sat more or less upright with one leg tucked away and "skulled" herself across the polished floors with the other one. Her mother would exclaim to visitors, "Come and see my daughter! Isn't she a silly!" The little girl would then perform to everyone's delight. When she stood up she received no applause at all since this was the kind of thing that children of her age should do, instead she was seriously coaxed to walk. Her immediate reaction was to sit down and draw the laughs.

The mother was quite genuinely anxious to teach the child to walk and she covered her anxiety by pretending that she appreciated the funny aspect of her daughter's backwardness. She provided powerful reinforcement for the sliding and none for the walking. It should be added that the girl is now an extremely attractive graduate with an unimpeachable shape.

Children who do not like school will have their attitude reinforced by teachers who keep them in as a punishment. When the author taught in

14

schools he allowed children to stay in for an hour or so on two evenings a week as a reward for good work. So successful was this that any child who was kept out of school after school hours showed every indication of being severely punished.

The fact that unwitting conditioning takes place and that it can lead to reorientation of attitudes means that it must be recognized and planned for. A sales training room, for example, should reflect the "image" which the company wants to attract to its products. Special attention should be paid to the first impressions which students receive on entering the training room and to the last ones they receive as they leave it.

A sales training department in the motor industry decided to sell a particular car on, among other grounds, its elegance. The sales training room was therefore designed to reflect this concept in a restrained fashion. The instruction was supported by elegant illustrations tastefully and efficiently presented and at the end of each day the final summary was an elegant visual one on a felt board which occupied a dominant position.

Examples are without number. Science teachers should be known to have a scientific attitude, teachers of printing should prepare their chalkboard layouts with special care and understanding, chalkboards should not be used in a metrology laboratory or the concern for cleanliness will make little impact and so on.

TEACHING FOR STRUCTURING INSIGHTS

Sometimes the learner is faced with the need, as it were, to put two and two together; to build up an understanding from a number of understood concepts and known facts. In this situation the teacher will provide and assemble the data and then allow opportunities for the new understanding to form. As an example, let us suppose that students are to be taught to manipulate and understand quadratic expressions. The sequence might take the form shown on page 16 (*Fig. 7*).

The students are then told to copy the diagram and write the equation and then to draw five others and give their meanings in symbols.

In this example the students put together their previously formed concepts of squares and rectangles, of area and addition, of facts like $xy + xy = 2xy$ and manipulate them until they form the new concept of the quadratic expression. Notice too that they work from concrete things to the abstractions which they represent and they work from particular cases until they are ready to generalize.

TEACHING BY EVOKING INVOLVEMENT

There are occasions when the dominant factor in learning appears to be the absorption of the learner in his task and there is some problem-solving

T Here is a square *(Fig. 7).* Its side is . . . well . . . I don't know its length so I will call it *x*. Since this side is *x*, this side is . . .*x*, and the area of the square is . . . ?

S x^2.

This represents x^2

FIG. 7(*a*)

T Good. I will put the area of x^2 here. (Putting it on a magnetic board.) And here is a rectangle. You can see the length of this side?

S *x*.

T Good, and the length of this side . . . I don't know *that* either so I will call it *y*. Length *x*, breadth *y*, so its area is?

S *xy*.

This represents $x^2 + xy$

FIG. 7(*b*)

T Good. I will put this alongside the x^2 making the total area?

S $x^2 + xy$

S $x^2 + 5xy + 6y^2$

T The length of this final rectangle is?

S $x + 3y$.

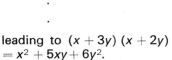

leading to $(x + 3y)(x + 2y)$
$= x^2 + 5xy + 6y^2$.

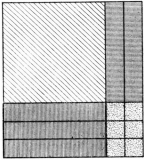

This represents $x^2 + 5xy + 6y^2$

FIG. 7(*c*)

to which this involvement seems to be the key. It is initiated by a challenge made introspectively by the learner, one which in its turn may be evoked by a challenge set by his teacher. The teacher's contribution alone is not enough: the learner must respond to the goadings of his own challenge which depends in turn upon his self-esteem.

16

The kind of tension this creates may be experienced by attempting to solve the following code in which any number can be represented by letters. As you try it notice the sequence of attitudes beginning with a fairly confident one during which a hopeful clue is found, tested and assessed. If it results in a solution, the experience gives you a sense of relaxed well-being. If not, you hesitate and then approach the problem again with greater caution seeking another clue. Once found, this too is tested and so on. Notice that the clues are insights which may or may not be reliably structured and notice too that they seem to develop suddenly. If you cannot solve the problem you tend to become less intelligent in your approach to it—particularly if you are being watched by a person in authority—until ultimately you reject the problem and want to reject the person who set it.

Number	Symbol	Number	Symbol	Number	Symbol
0	z	16	dq	64	uqq
1	u	17	dc	71	ucc
2	d	18	tz	72	dzz
3	t	19	tu	108	tzz
4	q	20	td	109	tzu
5	c	24	qz	110	tzd
6	uz	29	qc	111	tzt
7	uu	30	cz	148	qzq
8	ud	35	cc	180	ctd
10	uq	37	uzu	215	ccc
11	uc	38	uzd	216	uzzz
12	dz	41	uzc	220	uzzq
13	du	42	uuz	432	dzzz
14	dd	48	udz	468	duzz
15	dt	49	udu	500	ducd

The teacher who wants to initiate involvement will structure his presentation with this end in view. Here, for example, is the conclusion of a lesson to nineteen-year-old student engineers given the week before they learn Bernoulli's theorem (*Fig. 8*):

Teacher: I have here a piece of cardboard with a pin through it. If I hold it and then let it go (demonstrates) it falls down.

And here is a cotton reel with a hole through it. If I put the pin in the hole in the cotton reel, hold it and then let go of the cardboard (demonstrates), it falls down.

But if I put the pin in the hole in the cotton reel and blow down the hole to blow the cardboard away (demonstrates), the harder I blow the tighter the cardboard clings to the reel. Now for homework I want you to explain why this happens.

17

This has proved to be one of the author's most successful pieces of teaching: let us analyse it.

The first two demonstrations considerably redress the balance of superiority in the room. This leads the students to feel relaxed and confident. But they also feel a little nettled by the unsophisticated nature of the equipment. But in the third stage of the presentation they know (since three is a number of some significance in this context) that a kind of crisis has been reached and something unexpected is going to happen and consequently they attend

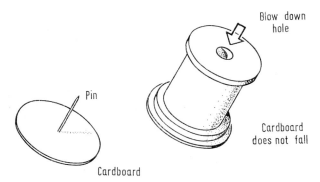

Blow down hole

Pin

Cardboard does not fall

Cardboard

Fig. 8. Demonstration equipment for problem involving Bernoulli's Theorem

closely. When, in the end, the problem is stated they feel determined to solve it:

(a) because it is about such simple things (indeed feminine things) that they cannot face being beaten by it;

(b) because they were made to feel superior before the critical question was asked. (How difficult to say "I don't know," when someone asks for directions to somewhere!)

It can confidently be assumed that they would go home and repeat the demonstration in a quiet place and then, having satisfied themselves that there was no trick would find out all they could on the subject in order to avoid any similar discomfort when the class next met.

Notice that in this communication, there seems to be no connexion between what the teacher does and says and the process of conditioning; that he acts as a catalyst, triggering off an introspectively set challenge; that this can bear fruit only if the learner is allowed to devote himself to finding the solution he needs.

So much for the background. From where the teacher stands, learning does not always seem to result from the same set of causes. On some occasions the prime mover in learning seems to be the process of conditioning, on others it seems to consist of a need to fit together experiences and ideas to make a new pattern of understanding, on yet others it seems to be a response to challenge; a challenge set introspectively and seen against the learner's private estimate of his own potential level of achievement. These pressures which lead to learning will be deployed advantageously by the skilled teacher who recognizes the psychological adjustments that learners are likely to make to developing learning situations. As he teaches he reduces all his studies of learning theory to such convenient, if superficial, shorthand in order to make appropriate adjustments and manoeuvres at the operational level.

People, he keeps in mind, learn when they are able to learn and when they want to learn. And, although they are not basically separable, the tactics he uses are based on the assumptions that learning results from conditioning or from the structuring of insights or from the pressure of an introspective challenge.

REFERENCES

1. THORNDIKE, E. L., *Animal Intelligence*, London, Macmillan, 1911.
2. THOMSON, ROBERT, *The Psychology of Thinking*, London, Pelican.
3. DEUTSCH, J. A., *The Structural Basis of Behaviour*, Cambridge, 1960.
4. OLDS, J., Hypothalamic Substrates of Reward, *Psychological Review*, 42, 554, London, 1962.
5. SKINNER, B. F., *The Behaviour of Organisms*, New York, Appleton-Century-Crofts Inc., 1938.
6. FERSTER, C. B., and SKINNER, B. F., *Schedules of Reinforcement*, New York, Appleton-Century-Crofts, Inc., 1957.

FURTHER READING

BORGER, ROBERT, and SEABOURNE, A. E. M., *The Psychology of Learning*, London, Penguin Books, 1966.

The Penguin Modern Psychology Series, particularly
Animal Problem Solving (UPS7), *Attitudes* (UPS3), *Motivation* (UPS11), and *Thinking and Reasoning*.

2 PERCEPTION

It is convenient to divide the process of communication into separate stages in order to examine its different characteristics in greater detail. Communication begins at a source, an object, say, or an idea in the mind of a person, and from this source, the information contained in the communication is transmitted to the receiver. During its transfer this information may be in the

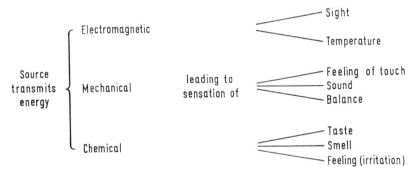

FIG. 9. Communication involves the transmission and conversion of energy

form of light radiation, radio waves, sound, liquid droplets and so on, but whatever form it takes it transfers energy from the source to the nerve endings of the receiver (*Fig.* 9). If the receiver is unconscious the process ends here and cannot properly be called communication, but a healthy conscious person absorbs this communication energy on his skin (and calls it feeling) on his taste buds (and calls it smell or taste), on the retina of his eye (and calls it seeing), or on the drum of his ear (and calls it hearing).

At the nerve endings the energy is converted from light, sound, compression or chemical energy into electrical energy and, in this form it is transferred along nerves to the brain where the information it contains is abstracted.[1] This is the stage at which perception occurs (*Fig.* 10) and because the relationship between the form and structure of the communication and the person who receives it can considerably affect perception we are going to examine this process more closely.

20

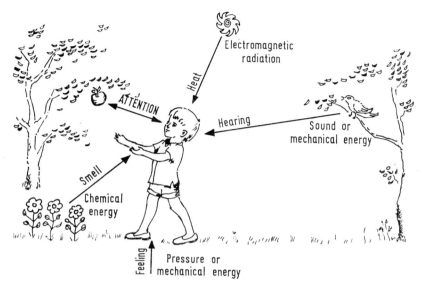

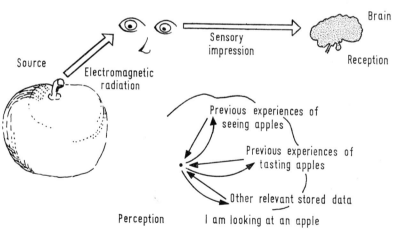

Electromagnetic
radiation

Heat

ATTENTION

Hearing

Sound or
mechanical energy

Smell

Chemical
energy

Feeling

Pressure or
mechanical energy

(a) Attention is selective awareness

Source

Electromagnetic
radiation

Sensory
impression

Brain

Reception

Previous experiences of
seeing apples

Previous experiences of
tasting apples

Other relevant stored data

Perception   I am looking at an apple

(b) Attention leads to perception

FIG. 10. Perception is an active response to communication

ATTENTION

Let us first recall the kind of analysis of communications data that occurs in the brain. Suppose, for example, we are talking to a friend in a room crowded with people. We follow what the friend is saying but all the other conversations merge into a kind of grey noise. Obviously, our reception can be selective: we can pay attention to one stream of stimuli to the apparent exclusion of others: we discriminate. But if one of the chatterers includes our name in his conversation, or uses a word to which we normally respond energetically we notice it and begin dividing our attention between the conversation to which we were originally tuned and this new source of interest. Noticing the critical word or phrase may not be instantaneous: a few seconds may elapse before we are fully aware of what has been said. Thus the brain is obviously not tuned into one conversation to the total exclusion of all others as a radio might be, but rather is it responding actively to one source and passively to the others. This active response to communication in which the brain reaches out, as it were, after meaning, is the prerequisite of perception. Facts are learned by sensing and discriminating in this way. The passive response is a relaxed seemingly effortless awareness of a background.

The same kind of focusing characterizes the reception of communication in its other forms. We may look analytically at a small picture on a wall and this appears to occupy our entire visual effort. But, at the same time, we know that the wall itself, the floor and ceiling and so on are imaged on the retinas of our eyes. We appear to take no notice of them at all. But if the carpet started rising from the floor, or a shadow moved across the ceiling we would immediately attend to it: the more apparently menacing the movement, the more energetic would our reaction to it be.

This passive awareness of fields of sound, sight, smell, taste and feel is part of our personal defence system which has ensured the survival of our species: the focused attention is this and more; it is the entrance through which we receive the raw material of what we know.

At the onset then, an individual may attend to sensory impressions or he may ignore them. If he ignores them they become part of the communications background or "noise" whilst if he attends he does so because he is motivated by interest or fear and his brain responds to them actively by reaching out for their meaning.

Thus when a teacher is communicating, his first task is to attract and hold the attention of his learners. If students do not attend, the teacher's talking and illustration become noise. If the students do attend, however, their brains will attempt to relate the information they receive with ideas they already possess and they will attempt to simplify and generalize it.

Although it is outside the scope of this work to dwell on the physiological processes which are initiated by attention, an appreciation of their complexity may ward off tendencies to believe in such slick panaceas as, "If you attend to me you will understand!"

22

Our knowledge of the activities which occur in the nervous system and the brain has grown with the development of microelectrodes with diameters less than a ten-thousandth of an inch capable of contacting single cells and of detecting electrical potentials of millionths of a volt. With these tools, Hubel and Wiesel of Harvard for example have shown that when we see, we in fact, code the inverted retinal image for colour, contour, and shape, a process which consists of the switching on or switching off of neurons by light falling on clearly defined areas on the retina. A particular neuron in the visual cortex may be switched on by a spot of light on one point and switched off by a similar spot on another point. Others respond to lines of light but not to spots and then only to lines in a particular orientation. The retina is therefore a matrix of excitatory and inhibitory areas and not a sensing device like a photographic plate. Ragnar Granit and others in Sweden found that most of the cells in the photosensitive layer of the retina were activated by light from the entire visible spectrum whilst some were activated by light from a narrow band of frequencies. The former cells responded to overall brightness and the latter to colour. They have found too that the colour-selective process is not confined to the photosensitive ganglions but is supplemented by activities in cells between the pigment layer of the eye and the retina, and in the lateral geniculate bodies which respond selectively to the red-green on the one hand and the yellow-blue on the other. Seeing, then, is an electro-chemical coding and decoding process of a binary character which involves a series of sensing areas.

This account could continue, but sufficient has been said to show that beyond the reception of the sensory impression—and this is true of all the senses—an extraordinarily complex process of coding and decoding occurs. And, quite evidently, interference can come from a wide range of sources. Like the disturbances which affect the message before reception, this interference which occurs inside the receiver is also called noise, and of special interest in teaching is the misinterpretation of words which is due to semantic noise.

FACTORS INFLUENCING INTERPRETATION

The mode of communication which leads most easily to successful understanding will, in general, be preferred to other modes since we are motivated by experiences which appear directed towards success and discouraged by those which seem to be directed towards failure. And since there is a close link between intelligence and the efficiency of the physiological reactions to sensory impressions, preferred modes of communication will, broadly speaking, vary with intelligence.

The preferred mode of receiving the daily news for example can be educed from people's news-receiving habits. In general only those with a high intelligence read quality newspapers. Their choice derives from their ability

23

to understand unillustrated verbal information in which words are selected to give precise nuances of meaning irrespective of their difficulty. These people prefer to receive information in the form of technical words, abstractions, and generalizations, which give a great deal of precise information in a small compass. The average person reads popular newspapers in which the news is illustrated by photographs and expressed in commonplace words and simple sentences. He prefers to receive information in the form of particular cases—"the attack on blonde mother-of-five, Mrs. Jessie Smith of . . ." rather than police statistics—and concrete examples—"your beer will cost a penny more a pint" rather than abstract ones such as cost-of living indices. He also likes to see who is telling him the news and is therefore better able to attend to difficult information on television than in a newspaper or on the radio. The person of low intelligence does not read news at all but he likes line drawings of the strip-cartoon variety. He understands best by doing things—when he has "a go" himself. To him unemployment statistics are meaningless, photographs of unemployed make little impact: it is being unemployed that has meaning.

These different news-receiving characteristics derive from the different levels of ability to perceive. The intelligent man is able to match new information against his vast store of facts and concepts and find associations, connexions and similarities which the unintelligent man cannot. Thus the useful component in the statement that "the world is like an orange" could be abstracted only by somebody with a sufficient experience of oranges *and* worlds *and* similarities, and to most people the words, "There is a green hill far away without a city wall" can mean only that the hill, which is green and far away has not a city wall around it. Since no hills in their experience ever had city walls around them the words are relegated to mouth movements which accompany a tune. A photograph would clarify the statement for some whilst a selective line drawing would make the idea clear to most.

The intellectual search for interconnexions which goes on at a high level of intelligence can be appreciated in the following example. A group of people were given a lecture on the principles of the operation of a gas refrigerator. This was fully illustrated with models, diagrams and so on and carefully planned to be the most efficient instrument of communication possible within the framework set by the lecturing technique. Some hours later one of the audience—a highly intelligent arts graduate—gave this account of what she had learned:

Refrigeration by Gas

The problem is to understand how heat can produce cold. The atoms of a solid substance are arranged in a pattern; in a liquid they are disorganized; in a gas they fan out and bombard any container. Energy is produced by heat. Evaporation causes cooling. When water boils it evaporates quickly, but its temperature remains constant. Other substances evaporate

24

quickly at room temperature, e.g. ether. Ammonia is a substance that evaporates quickly—I am not sure at what temperature. A gas refrigerator consists of a number of small containers linked by tubes. These form a system of circuits. Ammonia is heated so that it evaporates. The vapour so formed passes up a tube at the top of which is a container where it condenses as ice.

Not all the vapour passes up this vertical tube. Some passes along a horizontal tube until it permeates a container of water. This water becomes impregnated with ammonia vapour. As a consequence it forms a gas which returns to the original container of ammonia and condenses back into liquid ammonia. There is clearly a gap in my exposition. I cannot have been attending very well at this point. I believe that somehow the ice gives off water vapour which is drawn downwards and condenses as water—the water which is then impregnated with ammonia.

Why does all this movement take place? I think it is because water has a greater density than ammonia, and therefore the lighter gas moves towards the heavier liquid. When the water is transformed by the ammonia solution it becomes light and mobile; it is then drawn back to the liquid ammonia container.

Here the effort to find meaning is sustained—a characteristic of high intelligence—but the success diminishes as the complexity of the demand increases. Where the patterns which the communication attempted to evoke required a structure of scientific knowledge which the learner did not possess, she drew upon ideas which seemed to provide the best match. At first these are sufficient—"ammonia is a substance that evaporates quickly," "ammonia condenses as ice," "water becomes impregnated with ammonia vapour." But then the store gives out: "As a consequence it forms a gas and returns to the original container of ammonia," "therefore the lighter gas moves towards the heavier liquid," "water is transformed by the ammonia."

Another characteristic of the seeker after meaning is brought out by this passage: "There is clearly a gap in my exposition . . . I cannot have been attending very well at this point." The receiver who does not understand appreciates that the communicator knows what he is attempting to communicate and this creates a psychological imbalance of superiority. The receiver feels that the relative inadequacy of his relevant knowledge is the sole cause of the communications breakdown. This submission on the receiver's part feeds back to the transmitter who is persuaded that the receiver is indeed the culprit. From a professional point of view breakdown in communication during teaching is always the responsibility of the teacher: it means he is not providing sufficiently for the perceptual abilities of his students.

PERCEPTION AND LEARNING

When perception results from greater effort it tends to persist longer whether

25

Fig. 11. Overhead projector sequence illustrating perceptual development

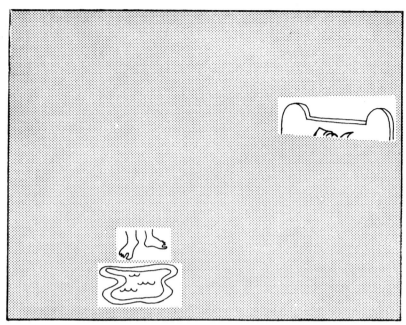

FIG. 11 (cont.)

it is accurate or not. This tendency to persist is considerably increased by a little reinforcement. This may be demonstrated by the following example.

A simple picture (*Fig.* 11) is shown in stages with a few seconds' interval between each stage. As a result of making an active response to the visual sensations, the viewer interprets and verbalizes what he sees. If the second small part of the picture fits in with his interpretation of the first, his perception is reinforced so strongly that he expects the subsequent sections to fit in with his construct. In other words his own perceptual creation of what the picture is like takes a kind of precedence over the picture itself. In the face of sufficient evidence of the inaccuracy of his first construction, the viewer may become disheartened and give up attending.

The usual reactions to viewing this particular sequence are:

1. These are a pair of feet I think; probably boy's feet—a little boy,
2. *and* (this is significant in that it implies a confirmation of the first decision) this is a pool of water. This is a little boy fishing in a pool.
3. Bother! This doesn't fit. I'll leave this until I have more information.
4. Expressions of surprise.

In receiving the first part of a set of new information the brain tries to find a background into which details will fit with precision: rationalizing this drive makes scientists. If this is not provided it will be created and if the details appear to reinforce the initial perceptual creation, it will tend to persist even in the light of contrary evidence. The following sequence is a possible perceptual construct from spoken communication:

"Two raised to the power of one is two"
(If two is multiplied by one I get two.) Tentative.

"Two raised to the power of two is four."
(If two is multiplied by two I get four.) Confirmatory.

"Two raised to the power of three is eight."
(This must be wrong.) Hesitant.

"Two raised to the power of four is sixteen."
(This is beyond me: I'll never understand.) Regression.

In each example the particular difficulty of rogue perception—of creating something that is not there—could be eliminated by giving the learner a vague general idea of the whole at the onset. This, in the latter, might take the form of "$2 \times 2 \times 2 \times 2 \times 2$ is called two raised to the power of five because five twos are multiplied together, etc."

An interesting experiment which bears out the persistence of decisions in the light of contrary evidence was reported in the *American Journal of Physics*.[2] Pupils who did not know the answers and who were aged between seven and twelve years were asked to predict which of two objects would reach the floor first if they were dropped from the ceiling simultaneously: one was substantially heavier than the other. Most of the pupils predicted that the heavier one would reach the floor first. When the weights were dropped and, to the demonstrator, quite obviously reached the ground together, most of the pupils confirmed the prediction they had made. This type of test can be repeated with adults and the same results obtained. Craftsmen will insist on the superiority of a particular technique even in the face of contrary evidence. The author asked a group of woodworking apprentices which arrangement of nails would hold two pieces of wood together more permanently; a dovetail arrangement or a vertical arrangement (*Fig.* 12). They all predicted that

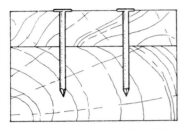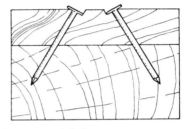

FIG. 12. Which is the stronger join?

the dovetail arrangement would be best. Testing with loads showed the vertical arrangement to be superior in most cases but the experiment was viewed with suspicion as being "artificial."

Some communications result, not in the creation of a perceptual response which is accurate or inaccurate, but in indecision as to what construction to accept. This too leads to frustration. The statement, "A number, which multiplied by itself, equals minus one" may result in this kind of indecision, as may the pictures in *Fig.* 13.

Notice that this indecision occurs at the perceptual level: an inability on the part of the brain to solve with any permanency, coded sensory impressions and naturally this indecision must be resolved before any concepts can be constructed. The former difficulty may be resolved by avoiding the words, "A number . . ." and substituting, "The symbol *j* multiplied by . . .," whilst the latter may be resolved by shading.

Whilst contemplating the perceptual confusion elicited by the illustration it is well to accept that artists (who draw for perceptual ends) are usually better qualified to produce "telling" visual aids than are technical draughtsmen who follow a precisely defined procedure irrespective of the visual impression it may evoke.

Notice too, the binary character of perceptual decisions. We can see a cube sticking out towards us or a cubical hole but, because we have learned

29

to recognize such a visual message as cubical, we cannot see it for what it is—a flat pattern of lines on a flat piece of paper.

Typical of research findings into the factors which influence perception is the work of Abercrombie.[3] Medical students, for example, were asked to look at and report on the same X-ray plate and out of some groups of twelve students there were twelve different interpretations of what was seen.

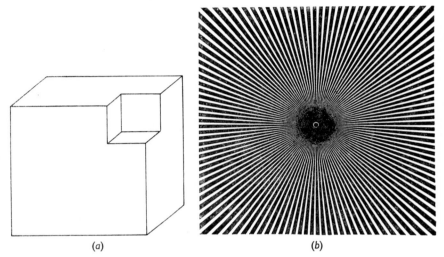

(a)   (b)

FIG. 13. Is the small cube in (a) an addition or a piece missing or is this a flat pattern of lines? Notice that (b) will not settle to a static image

The students then freely discussed their findings and, as a consequence, exposed to themselves the factors which influenced them in what they saw.

The author, at the end of group discussions, and in the absence of a verbal summary, has asked adult teachers-in-training to write down the most important findings of the group. A wide spread of interpretations was common with a strong tendency for individuals to give prominence to their own contributions.

In another experiment, groups were shown the picture (*Fig. 14*) and asked to write down what they saw. Salesmen and business students tended to see it as a layout of a factory or housing estate, printers as part of a mechanism and chemists as something to do with a computer or calculating machine. When it was shown to be the word THE (by fitting a black line along the top and bottom of the letters) the original interpretation seemed naïve and the outline could not be seen as anything other than THE even after the black lines were again removed.

Perceiving is the process of fitting together a jumble of sensations and finding a meaningful pattern, and it *may* lead to perceiving the idea the communication was intended to convey. There will, however, always be an unconscious bias towards perceiving what we have become accustomed to perceive—the ability to perceive is learned. To take a visual example. *Fig.* 15 shows a row of round-headed rivets: turn it upside down and it

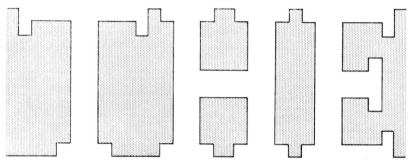

FIG. 14. A problem of perception

becomes a row of holes. We have become so accustomed to light coming from above that we therefore tend to interpret pictures as though this were invariably true. For the same kind of reason, beer tastes less pleasant in a breakfast cup than it does in a beer glass.

Learned perceptual traits reflect environmental characteristics. Most of us live in a world abounding with rectangles—one of the products of civilization—and, in general, these throw a trapezoidal image on the retinas of our

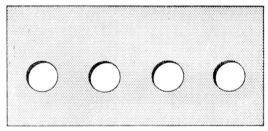

FIG. 15. We are accustomed to shadows beneath solids; turn this picture upside down and the bumps will become holes

eyes (*Fig.* 16 (*a*)). When, therefore, the data reaching our brains are consistent with a trapezoidal retinal image, we tend, in the absence of a conflicting frame of reference, to perceive a rectangle. A *rotating* trapezoidal frame (*Fig.* 16 (*b*)) is interpreted as a swinging *rectangular* window (Ames, 1951).[4] Zulus, who live in a non-rectilinear environment are much less likely to experience this inaccurate perception (Allport and Pettigrew, 1957).[5]

These three aspects of perceiving—the tendency to perceive with precision only when we know what we should perceive, to perceive what we anticipate

31

and to perceive what we have learned to perceive—are of consequence in single-channel communication since other channels usually provide either frames of reference against which the data can be matched or clues as to the information they carry. Indeed, a rotating trapezoidal frame projected from a silent film would be seen as a swinging rectangular frame by learners with insufficient knowledge of what the producer had in mind when he produced the film, whilst the producer would perceive the dynamic image as a rotating trapezoid because he knows already what to perceive. Learners could be induced to

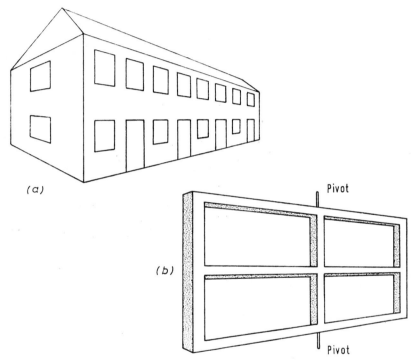

(a)

(b)

Pivot

Pivot

Fig. 16. Our rectilinear world (a) determines our interpretation of the rotation of (b)

perceive correctly by fitting the rotating frame on to a familiar device that always rotates or by adding a sound commentary to the film. The person who always writes the word *liaison* as *liason* sees it spelt that way when he reads it in print because that is what he anticipates. The written word *minimum* would be seen as the word *maximum* by a reader who expected it to be the word *maximum*. In demonstrating a beating action in elevation the teacher must expect those who believe it should be a circular motion to see it as one whilst those who believe it should be a linear motion will see it that way. This is of importance in film-making, demonstration work and lecturing to large groups.

Perceptual decisions are affected by the decisions of other people. In one of many experiments, a college of education staff were asked to assess the level of cultural ability of students from data which had been prepared in the form of histograms. These had to be given a rating on a five-point scale. When four of a group of five assessors deliberately marked high, the fifth one lowered his standard to fall into line. The visual sensation which, unbiased he would decode as average, he decoded as rich. Again this process occurs at the stage of perception—the reaching out after meaning stage—and not at the later stage of concept formation. This kind of social pressure becomes most marked in groups in which greater age or greater status creates a barrier to very free communication.

Perception is the mental decoding of sensations: it is an active response to communication in which the brain reaches after meaning.

We respond actively to sensations to which we attend: we are passively aware of all other sensations as part of our survival mechanism.

The physiological processes consequent upon attending to a sensation are highly complex and offer a correspondingly wide opportunity for interference by "noise" originating from both physical and psychological sources.

Perceptual ability depends upon intelligence, age and ability, environment, social pressure and so on.

The ability to perceive is learned as well as inherited. Perception may be efficient without being accurate: it is reinforced by sensations of success.

Reliable perception is more likely as the number of communications channels is increased.

One of the teacher's major tasks is to provide for accurate and efficient perception.

REFERENCES

1. LOWENSTEIN, OTTO, *The Senses*, London, Pelican, 1966.
2. CUNNINGHAM, JOHN and KARPLUS, R., Free Fall Demonstration Experiment, *American Journal of Physics*, Vol. 30, No. 9, p. 656, 1962.
3. ABERCROMBIE, M. L., *The Anatomy of Judgment*, London, Hutchinson, 1960.
4. AMES, A. JR., Visual Perception and the Rotating Trapezoidal Window, *Psychological Monographs*, 65, 32, 1951.
5. ALLPORT, G. W. and PETTIGREW, T. F., Cultural Influence on the Perception of Movement: the Trapezoidal Illusion among Zulus, *J. Abnorm. Soc. Psychol.*, 55, 104, 1957.

ADCOCK, C. J., *Fundamentals of Psychology*, London, Penguin, 1964.
FOSS, BRIAN M. (Ed.) *New Horizons in Psychology*, London, Penguin, 1966.
GREGORY, R. L., *Eye and Brain—the Psychology of Seeing*, World Universal Library, London, Weidenfeld & Nicolson, 1966.
VERNON, M. D., *The Psychology of Perception*, London, Penguin, 1962.

Penguin Modern Psychology Series, particularly
Attitudes (UPS3), *Experiments in Visual Perception* (UPS2), and *Nature of Emotion* (UPS12).

THE PROCESS IN ACTION

3　LEARNING IN SMALL GROUPS

This chapter is concerned with communication within groups of up to about a dozen members who are brought together in order to learn. This limit is chosen so that the kind of formality which size imposes upon larger groups need not concern us at this stage. It sets out to demonstrate that methods— the project method, tutorial method and so on—are merely structures and it is the communication patterns which those structures support that make them more or less useful devices for learning. Of course, it is possible to lecture to one person as though he were an audience of a hundred, but we are not concerned with the rarer occupational abnormalities from which instructors sometimes suffer.

CHARACTERISTICS OF A SMALL GROUP

The size of group may be limited in order to provide better learning conditions or because larger groups are not possible, but, in either case, the intellectual responses which its members make to their instructor and to one another will differ in character from what they would be in a larger group. The special feature of a small group is the degree to which members come to know one another in the context of the particular learning with which the group is concerned. This is not characteristic of a class of twenty or more which is always treated as a whole, since such groups will contain a number of well-defined sub-groups and within a group of this size the more introverted members can evade publicity; the true small group is the antithesis of the large lecture meeting where members tend to remain anonymous.

The "methods" employed with small groups include tutorials, seminars, group discussions, lessons, syndicates, case studies, role-playing and business games of various kinds, but the common factor which distinguishes them from large classes and lecture groups is the face-to-face communication which brings personalities into the open and involves members in active and public expression of their learning as it is taking place. This is not to say that these methods are "better" than others—they may well be economically wasteful in certain situations—but simply that psychologically they present learning

35

problems of different kinds. From the teacher's point of view they are "us learning" rather than "telling them."

Four main features of small-group learning must be allowed to weigh with the instructor:

1. The group will quickly arrive at a standard to which it will work.
2. It can easily become antagonistic towards outsiders.
3. A hierarchy will tend to become established.
4. In certain circumstances small groups can quickly accept false conclusions before which individuals would hesitate.

We shall consider each item in turn.

ROLE OF THE TEACHER

A small group brought together regularly for the purpose of learning will quickly develop certain well defined characteristics, most important of which is the "sentiment of liking" which grows up among them.[1] From this beginning group norms will be established and it is with these norms that the teacher must be concerned since they set the level of aspiration and effort for most of the group members. His contribution should centre upon raising these norms and maintaining them at realistically high levels so that, in unwittingly responding to the social pressures of the group, individual attainments will rise to correspond. This process of setting group standards as a catalyst for the changing of individual standards has a history of success. Perhaps the most homely comparison was made in the United States during the war against the Nazis when it was decided to persuade housewives to serve offal for meals. Hitherto, liver had been regarded as unsavoury—part of the "insides"—and the task might be compared with persuading British housewives to serve boiled intestines! The programme consisted of two alternative approaches: on the one hand attractively illustrated and well-informed lectures in which the nutritional value of these foods was emphasized, and on the other, guided group discussions leading to a group decision on the value of such foods as part of a normal diet. The group discussion method achieved a very much greater success rating than the lecture method.

A teacher who accepts low levels from a small group will find that individuals make no particular effort to exceed this level, indeed the group norm may even become established around the irrelevance and stupidity of the group achievement and individuals may suffer a repression of their educational aspirations. Although such behaviour is called indiscipline it is an acceptance of a standard and not the rejection of one and consequently the taking of disciplinary action is comparable to attempting to cure the patient by suppressing evidence of the symptoms. Only by raising the group norm can a "cure" be effected, since the value which an individual places upon himself

36

is measured by the attitudes towards him of the others whom he likes: these attitudes make "him" and are therefore his standards.

A teacher of a small group must therefore predict a level of performance for that group which is at once high and realistic. Except for the "rebel" each individual's self-esteem will be enhanced by the social approval of the group and as a consequence it is important, both that none should be discouraged by anticipating failure to meet the group standards and that each should associate the group with high endeavours.

The sentiments of liking which grow up between members of a group will be heightened and will give more satisfaction if they are accompanied by a dislike of others. The bonds holding a close-knit group may owe their initial strength to the liking which comes from the frequency of meeting but they may be consolidated by a dislike of, say, the police, the staff, Tories, the bosses, or the full-timers. This dislike may, indeed, continue to maintain the coherence of the group long after its original purpose for coming together has ceased to exist: in education it can more than offset the advantage of working in a small group if it develops around antisocial sentiments.

The second task of the group leader then, is to divert the group's dislike of those outsiders who stand for constructive or socially valuable influences to a dislike for destructive and antisocial influences, or to redirect it altogether into healthy competition. This latter procedure characterizes syndicate work and business games, but the author *has* seen respectable business men begin physically to fight over differences of opinion as to what constitutes proper conduct of groups during a business game.

As a group settles down, leaders will emerge and since group norms will be largely established by their leadership, their behaviour will tend to conform to the group behaviour pattern. Low ranking members, however, will tend to deviate from the norm and thus maintain or depress their status still more until a definite hierarchy is well established. Where this shows as a willingness to be led and leave all active participation to others the teacher must intervene. Despite this, the group influence as a whole usually results in a levelling out of progress: the group moves forward rather like a convoy of ships with the fastest member inevitably held back but enjoying the opportunity of sampling a wide variety of manoeuvres and exercises whilst the slowest works hard to keep up. No normal member of a small group wants to be too different from his colleagues.

Two characteristics of this kind of progress must be watched. There is, in general, an improvement in the *observable* aspects of progress at the expense of the others since social approval is earned through the former: for example, speed may improve at the expense of accuracy, or willingness to respond rather than to think. It is the teacher's task to ensure that the development of a mind which is alert to the needs of the moment must not be fostered at the expense of responsibility. Also, within small groups there is a tendency for individuals to agree with the majority, and since those who "know" speak out readily and with obvious confidence, they become the spokesmen for the group. It has been found that, as a result, logical problems tend to receive scant treatment; those who know, solve them and the majority pay only a little attention to the problems and practically none to the process of solving them: they wait for the solutions. Where human problems are concerned, however, there is more interaction and more attention from everyone; decisions are delayed because the wiser members are tentative in the face of such problems and correspondingly more weight attaches to the contributions of the slower members. Unfortunately, the same pattern obtains when those who speak out with confidence give *wrong* facts or misleading opinions—a wrong "solution" to a logical problem can be reached quickly and confidently and then become an impediment to further progress; an unacceptable "solution" to an open-ended problem impedes the development of clear thinking rather than contributing to the growth of subject knowledge.

SMALL GROUP PRODUCTIVITY

Experiments, such as those by Gibb,[2] show that the productivity of an unled group increases as its size decreases, productivity being measured in terms of the number of contributions of useful information and solutions to the problem undertaken. In larger groups, individuals tend to feel more inhibited. This changing pattern of intercommunication is observable down to unled groups of as few as three and four, with groups of eight and more often throwing up forceful and repressive leaders who reduce their colleagues to a state of relative docility.

Not only, then, does the smaller group offer more proportion of contribution time to each member, but it also provides a more encouraging climate than the larger group. And although by evening out the amount of contribution which members of larger groups make, tutors can offset the overt evidence of regression, the same emotions are at work behind the scenes.

The advantages which have been found for groups of two, three or four can be exploited so long as there is sufficient control over the general direction in which they make progress. The obvious way of exercising this control is for the small group to meet a tutor from time to time and support or modify its views and solutions against his penetrating inquiry. This, one form of the tutorial system, is highly effective but expensive in staff time. Another is to require a number of small groups to discuss the same problem and then for each, through a spokesman, to present its views and solutions to a formal meeting comprising all of the groups—a plenary session. This is the syndicate method. Notice that this larger meeting must perform a dual role: as far as possible it must provide everyone with the decisions which every group has reached and it must act as a directing and—if necessary—correcting influence on everyone. In certain circumstances, this control may be automatic because of the maturity of the participants and the seriousness of their task, but generally a degree of psychological pressure is necessary. The plenary session might be attended by experts who will comment upon the group progress, the reports might be published for a wider circulation or a tape recording made of the contributions: if decisions appear to be of value or consequence to others they will be reached with a greater sense of responsibility.

COMPETITION AND CO-OPERATION

It is relevant here to take note of the findings of the relative values of competition and co-operation. Our society values competition and to a certain extent, aggression. Children are taught to "stand up for themselves" and encouraged to "get to the top" and so on. Unlike some other societies, we are conditioned to compete, to want to score marks, to work off grievances and the rest. The comprehensive analysis by Deutsch[3] and work by others shows that co-operatively motivated groups are happier and individuals belonging to them respect and consider one another's viewpoints, have a heightened sense of responsibility and are more productive than groups in which individuals compete. These findings are the main argument against the method of cumulative assessment of individual progress. In co-operating groups, contributions are cumulative and individuals are helped forward by their neighbours whilst in competing groups, individuals are anxious to restrict or decry the contributions which others make.

PROJECTS

One of the most successful patterns which evokes co-operation is called the project method, but its success lies in the co-operative communication implicit in the method and not in any special quality of the organization. Here, faced with a common interest of some special consequence, a class will be allowed to indulge that interest freely. The larger class group will fragment

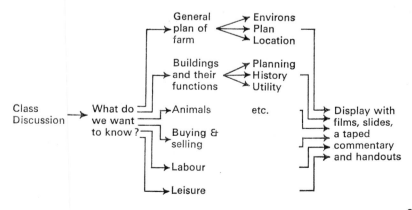

into small groups of twos and threes, each of which will undertake some component study from which the whole will subsequently be integrated. Typical of this method would be a study of a farm, for example (foot of p. 39).

As with any other method, the project method can be mishandled and fail to provide useful learning experiences. To succeed, it must be used in such a way as to exploit the opportunities it affords for freedom from the repression of aggressive leadership and for the acceptance by each small group of a responsible and unique role in the class society. To this end the purpose of the study should attract everyone in some way or another and each class member should move to that contributory task which he wants to perform. He should also work with those people towards whom he is attracted and he should be afforded opportunities for changing the task or his group in the light of his initial experiences. The direction should be provided unobtrusively by the tutor and the goal—be it an exhibition or a film, a book or a play—should provide the control. Although this appears excessively permissive, a high degree of self-discipline is established provided:

1. The tutor requires high but realistic standards to be reached by the group.
2. The small group contributions are essential components of the whole study.
3. The data, form and scope of the final expression of the study are precisely defined. The precision is essential to the exercise of control and the emergence of a full sense of group achievement.

ROLE-PLAYING

Role-playing is a method in which the learners act out the roles for which they are training. In salesmanship training, for example, one group member might play the role of a salesman and another the customer. The instructor will discuss a particular range of problems and situations and then select one of his trainees to interpret the lesson by acting as a salesman and another to act the prospect. Duplicated sheets will describe the selling situation and the "salesman" will leave the room to prepare his approach. The instructor will then brief the "customer" as to the character he should portray and the kinds of objections he will raise and he will ask the class to suggest ways of countering these objections.

The role-playing should now be enacted and afterwards the "salesman" asked to explain what he has done and where he could have been more successful. This will be followed by a discussion of the methods he has used and concluded by a second "salesman" playing the role in the light of the experiences he has accumulated.

This method clearly lends itself to irresponsibility. To offset this the standards set must again be high and co-operation must be encouraged at the expense of competition for self-esteem by scoring off colleagues. Again, a degree of permanence or publicity can press to this end.

To teach the rudiments of the binary system

Group: Technicians

Time: 35 minutes

Ideas upon which the choice of method is based.	Time (min.)	Matter	Method	Illustration
Introduction to give a general idea of the whole lesson and to motivate through interest.	0	Recap. of previous lesson "On-off" devices. Computers. Binary.	Questions, answers and explanations. (Face to face communications.)	Chalkboard heading.
Development (Behaviourist) rote learning for success.	4	"On-off" representation of numbers.	Educe from group: rote learning by Q and A. (Face to face communication.)	Magnetic board.
To provide data for insight formation.	8	Exercise on powers of two.	Class to complete duplicated exercise: individual help.	Duplicated sets of exercises.
Consolidation of data.	12	Powers of two in series.	Class to complete duplicated exercises: individual help.	Duplicated sets of exercises.
Insight formation.	16	Binary sequence.	Educe by Q and A. (Face to face.)	Magnetic board.
Application: possibility of regression through failure: give encouragement.	18	Exercise in translation to binary notation.	Class to complete duplicated exercises: individual help.	Duplicated sets of exercises.
Recapitulation and consolidation through enjoyment, activity and implications of relevance.	28	Adding by computer.	Role play: small group exercise.	
	35			Duplicated homework sheets.

(*See page* 44)

To introduce the subject of light

Group: G.1.

Ideas on which method is based.	Matter	Method	Chalkboard
To give general idea of whole. Focusing of attention.	Light is a form of energy.	*Demonstrate* candle, flint, lamp. *Question & answer. Discussion.*	Light is a form of energy.
To develop ability to observe.	Light can be converted into energy in other forms.	*Written* exercise. Individual attention.	
	Coloured light is obtained from white light.	*Demonstration* using filters.	
To consider two alternative hypotheses.	Either blue glass is transparent to blue light or it stains light blue.	*Exercise:* Class to complete diagram. *Demonstration:* Class represent observed data by diagrams. *Educe* staining filter theories.	
	Blue light is stopped by red glass—Why? Each glass absorbs light of all colours but its own colour: this it transmits.	*Discuss* and select filter theory.	

FIRST PEAK

- - - - - - - - - - - - - - - - -

To collect more relevant evidence concerning the relationship between light and colour.	The colour of a surface is the colour of the light it reflects: it absorbs light of other colours.	*Practical* exercise: Find which pair of filters transmit most light. Why? *Discuss.* *Demonstrate* with no explanation. Class to make diagram and explain.
SECOND PEAK To begin to resolve the complex of ideas.	Analysing white light.	*Practical* exercise with filters and coloured surfaces. *Demonstrate* with prism. *Discuss.*
THIRD PEAK To reach a general conclusion—the inductive step.		*Practical* exercise: Produce spectrum and try further dispersion with second prism. Produce white again. Pass spectrum over coloured card. *Observe* and explain.
Pointer to next lesson.	Revision and summary. Reference to further work.	*Filmstrip* with brief discussion.

White light consists of a series of coloured lights which form the SPECTRUM of white light.

(See page 44)

CASE STUDIES

Case studies should also involve small groups rather than large ones. Here, the group is presented with a problem and the way it was handled: an argument, say, between a workman and his foreman that ended in a strike.* This case might be role-played to the group by staff members, presented as a film or described on duplicated sheets and then freely discussed. Again, some kind of control is necessary and this can be provided by the decisions being incorporated in a role-play, filmed or outlined in a duplicated report.

LESSONS

The lesson, ideally will involve whatever methods seem to be most likely to provide the most beneficial opportunities for learning. It will be structured to establish and maintain interest, reduce fatigue (boredom) and encourage co-operation. Notes of lessons are given (pages 41–43). Notice that although lesson groups may not be small ones by our measure, the teacher employs techniques which enable him to take advantage of the values of small group communication.

In all of these cases the tutor's function is that of a guide. Experiments such as those of Maier and Solem[4] show that even with groups as small as five or six people, those whose chairman gave encouragement to the diffident, guidance to the hesitant and general leadership were more efficient and successful than those under a chairman who was completely permissive. Efficiency, however, should not be sought to the detriment of the cohesion of the group itself. A strongly cohesive group has a kind of momentum which is self-perpetuating: it even tends to pull in the non-conformist and, only when he is stubborn to the detriment of the group-effort will he be ignored. In such a group, friends will be more likely to agree than folk who like one another less.

MODES OF COMMUNICATION

The tutor, then, plays a major role in creating the climate for learning. He cannot shrug off the fact that he *is* the tutor and he can never become fully accepted as just another member of the group: he must always remain a kind of outsider. His attitude towards the group will become apparent through his manner of communicating with its members. He may adopt an authoritative approach in the interest of what appears to him to be simplicity and speed: he will *tell* members and show them what they should know. This appears to satisfy the need for order, efficiency and discipline, but it is based upon a false assumption: that group members can accept and live by impersonal rules. It aims at conditioning and readily leads to frustration, to increased hostility and aggression, and a decrease in the feedback of information to the tutor. It is frequently the sign of the tutor's feelings of

* A fine example of this type of film is "Dispute" by the British Productivity Council.

insecurity or of his need for personal gratification and it establishes a routine which cannot be relaxed without unwelcome reactions. Only for short-term specific situations such as operations involving danger is authoritative communication likely to be the most effective.

The tutor may use manipulative persuasion—a form of communication which is possible to people who are sensitive to human needs and emotions because it aims at using these needs as tools to exert influence. Its weakness shows in a lack of direction and of disorganized progress, of group members not being sure where they stand and feeling dependent upon the tutor because he or his prestige seems to depend upon them. Whilst authoritative communication is designed to threaten, manipulative communication is designed to seduce: both are likely to fail in the long term because of their built-in dishonesty of purpose.

Ideally the tutor should aim at collaborative communication; at providing learners with the means by which they may satisfy their needs through work. It places responsibility on the group and is concerned with inspiring, instructing and reporting: in providing learners with a knowledge of their progress as it is being made. At root, this is the basis of sound human relationships and of healthy motivation. Some valuable work on the relative effects of different modes of communication in learning was done by Lippitt and White with groups of eleven-year-old boys.[5]

To sum up, small groups of up to about a dozen members have the following characteristics which differ from those of large ones:

Members quickly come to like one another.

The group tends to dislike "outsiders."

It tends to develop a hierarchy.

It can readily reach false conclusions and accept them.

Smaller unled groups of three or four tend to be more efficient than larger ones of ten or eleven.

Co-operatively motivated groups are much more efficient than competitively motivated groups.

Small group working is exploited in "lessons", the project method, role-playing and case study methods, syndicate method and tutorial system.

The tutor's role is essential to efficient learning.

Authoritative communication from tutor to group aims to threaten, manipulative communication to seduce. For a healthy learning climate the communication mode should be collaborative and aim at providing individuals with the means of finding personal satisfaction through co-operative work.

REFERENCES

1. HOMANS, GEORGE C., *The Human Group*, London, Routledge & Kegan Paul, 1951.
2. GIBB, J. R., The Effect of Group Size and Threat Reduction upon Creativity in Problem Solving, *Amer. Psychol.* Vol. 6, 1951.
3. DEUTSCH, M., A Theory of Co-operation and Competition upon Group Progress, *Human Rel.*, Vol. 2, 1949.
4. MAIER, N. R. F. and SOLEM, A. R., The Contribution of the Discussion Leader to the Quality of Group Thinking, *Human Rel.*, Vol. 5, 1952.
5. NEWCOMB, T. M. and HARTLEY, E. L. (Eds.), *Readings in Social Psychology*, 2nd ed., New York, 1952.

FURTHER READING

ABERCROMBIE, M. L. J., *The Anatomy of Judgement*, London, Hutchinson, 1960.

BERGER, PETER L., *Invitation to Sociology*, London, Penguin, 1968.

BLACKBURN, R. and COCKBURN, A. (Eds.), *The Students' Revolt*, London, Penguin, 1969.

BRITISH INSTITUTE OF MANAGEMENT, MANAGEMENT TRAINING TECHNIQUES (conference), 68 pp., 1962.

CLEUGH, M. F., *Educating Older People*, London, Tavistock Publications, 1962.

JAHODA, M., *The Education of Technologists*, London, Tavistock Publications, 1963.

KIBBEE, JOEL M. and others, *Management Games: a new Technique for Executive Development*, 347 pp., Reinhold, 1961.

OTTERWAY, A. K. C., *Learning through Group Experience*, London, Routledge & Kegan Paul, 1966.

RICHARDSON, ELIZABETH, *The Environment of Learning*, London, Nelson, 1967.

SPROTT, W. J. H., *Human Groups*, London, Penguin, 1958.

4   LECTURING TO LARGE GROUPS

In short, over indulgence in being lectured to is a primrose path to intellectual sloth, the more fatally deceitful because it looks virtuous.
Sir Arthur Quiller-Couch: *A Lecture on Lectures:*   Hogarth Press: London, 1927.

Lectures were once useful; but now, when all can read, and books are so numerous, lectures are unnecessary.
Dr. Johnson: from Boswell, *Life of Johnson.*

The lecture is the most frequently and strongly criticized form of communication for learning.* Every tutor who discusses lectures with his students knows that much of their content is forgotten after a short interval of time. And yet the lecture persists.   Is it indeed too inefficient to be of value?

A series of experiments comparing the lecture and lesson techniques for introducing the binary system to adults carried out by the author gave results in favour of the lecture (despite the original intention of showing the superiority of the lesson!).   Following up the correspondence initiated by certain public lectures testifies to the very active response that they are capable of evoking.   Perhaps it is not the technique which is at fault but the purpose for which it is employed.

Those who condemn the lecture advocate more active participation by group members.   Josephine Klein in her book *Working with Groups*[1] opens her second chapter with the following anecdote:

> Two psychologists wrote to all those who had been present at a meeting of the British Psychological Society and asked them what they could remember of the recent discussion . . . only a tenth of the points that had been made were recalled in the reports.   Of these, nearly half were "substantially incorrect," . . .   The average member was, however, no more accurate about (points he had contributed) himself than he was about others.

---

* See for example Chapter 3 of *Educating Older People* by M. F. Cleugh, Tavistock Publications.

The opponents of lecturing hold that few people are capable of really good lecturing, that the lecture often invites insincerity and showing off on the part of the lecturer and posing on the part of the audience and, perhaps more important, that it does not fulfil a truly educative function since it represses the learner's initiative and reduces his role to that of a recipient of ideas instead of an active participant in their generation.

Many of the pronouncements made on the relative effectiveness of different modes of communication take no account of the widths of the spectra of abilities, subjects and circumstances. No critic would regard the physically passive audience at a symphony concert as ill-served nor would he assess the success of the performance by testing for the retention of certain phrases taken out of context. Some groups of ideas are akin to the coherent sequence in a symphony and can be presented only by sustained and delicately balanced arguments which are more readily comprehensible to some people when they are heard than when they are read. In such circumstances the lecture is an appropriate mode of presentation. Here the lecturer demonstrates how he, the master craftsman as it were, produces his masterpieces. He can show the sequence, draw attention to the pitfalls, highlight that which is of great significance because he knows so well. To chop up such a demonstration (by discussion technique, for example), however well the joints may be concealed, presents the audience with something different from the whole in the same way as a symphony played in instalments would be different in quality from the whole. At such a lecture the learners are responding to and developing the discipline which lies behind the capacity to be creative.

The Report of the University Grants Committee[2] on methods summarized the evidence in favour of lectures as follows:

> Immature university students learn more readily by listening than by reading.
> Lectures are especially valuable for introducing and opening up a subject and students can thus be led into subjects which would otherwise prove too daunting for them.
> It is easier to co-ordinate lectures (than tutorials, etc.) and laboratory work.
> Where knowledge is advancing rapidly textbooks may not be available.
> Lectures awaken a critical attitude in students.
> Lectures can provide aesthetic pleasure.
> Inspiring teachers, by lecturing, can infect far more students.
> Lectures are economical of staff time.

This report referred to university lectures in 1964 when ten per cent of groups attending lectures numbered less than five students and six per cent of groups were over one hundred. In the next year the Robbins Committee[3] stated it saw little value in formal lectures delivered to small audiences.

The American Committee on the Utilization of College Teaching Resources[4] did not support the widely held view that small classes were essential to the most efficient learning. It stated that "more students are capable of working independently of classroom instruction than have been given the opportunity . . . but they require to be prepared for independent study to get the fullest benefit from it." As part of this preparation for independent study, the Committee included lecturing to very large groups by good lecturers. It strongly recommended that every institution should be organized to provide for groups of a wide variety of sizes including very large ones. (*See also* references 5 and 6.)

As with kissing, clinical tests can prove that lecturing is a "bad thing." Indeed, the comparison can be taken further. Those who have never participated in a good lecture cannot know its power to inspire: its full impact can only be appreciated by consenting adults; its effectiveness is usually dependent in part upon effective visual aids. And, furthermore, despite all the protests, it is going to remain an important mode of communication for a considerable time to come.

The special quality of a successful lecture to a large group is the air of occasion which surrounds it—the size of the lecture hall, the shifting groupings of people, the shuffling hush of conversation which snuffs out as the proceedings begin, the vote of thanks and the applause. This is more than somebody talking to people. The lecture content too is special. It will have been prepared, rehearsed, arranged and, if necessary, spiced with verbal asides or illustrations. A lecture is often the culmination of the work of many people: those who prepare the hall, invite the audience, control the lighting, check the acoustics, introduce the lecturer and cope with the wide range of details which escape notice unless they are overlooked.

The successful lecturer will have learned certain abilities. He will be able to exploit the responses special to crowds—those strange responses of expectancy, humour, inspiration and the like which can be evoked only with large audiences and which have their roots in some incomprehensible form of communication so highly developed in certain kinds of gregarious animals. His response to his audience and his accommodation to his subject are the strategies of the craft, not the rules. The strategies are the lecturer's personal interpretations and although they may be modified by his knowing the rules by which he should lecture they are not determined by them.

The rules of lecturing, on the other hand, the guide-lines, are the procedures which are generally followed by successful lecturers. These include ways of structuring a lecture, how to stand and so on. But like the rules for happy marriages they may be broken by the most experienced of practitioners but should never be ignored by the novice.

THE PURPOSE OF A LECTURE

In a successful lecture a person and a particular area of his competence are presented to a willing audience which is capable of assessing them critically.

Matching the lecturer and his subject on the one hand with the audience on the other is essential to success since during a lecture there is no overt feedback from the listeners, and although able lecturers sense rapport, and make adjustments to maximize it as they lecture, they should not be forced to make major modifications to their prepared plan. This throws the initial responsibility for success on the organizer who, in addition to his function as a promoter and manager, must also bring together a lecturer and audience who are compatible one with the other.

The purposes for which lectures are particularly suitable are:

1. To give a general idea of the scope and content of a subject which is to be studied in detail later.
2. To stimulate interest in a subject or line of action or thought.
3. To present a new thesis or technique.
4. To persuade people of their own capacity to understand or enjoy; and
5. To provide an aesthetically stimulating experience and to quote the greatest of all lecturers—Michael Faraday: "A flame should be lighted at the commencement and kept alive with unremitting splendour to the end." (*Advice to a Lecturer*, Michael Faraday, The Royal Institution.)

LECTURE SETTINGS

No lecture is ever completely isolated as an experience although some may be unsupported by any formal preparation or recapitulation by the listeners. Such lectures, provided attendance at them is voluntary, and provided they are accurately advertised, can be stimulating sources of learning since, in general, they will be attended by audiences with an interest in the subject, or the speaker. Such lecture meetings should usually terminate with a discussion but, in general, this will serve only to clarify certain issues which were not quite clear to some people. This type of lecture, whilst it ostensibly provides information, should aim primarily at attitude-reinforcement. It caters for people who are interested enough to attend and are therefore likely to be willing to go further provided the lecture stimulates them to do so (*Fig.* 17). The contents of such lectures should be summarized in a handout or extended in a booklet. Often a bibliography will be valuable.

A lecture which is to be followed by seminars or group discussions* on the other hand can result in closely controlled learning (*Fig.* 18). Prior to the lecture, selected group leaders will be briefed by the lecturer so that the essential content of his presentation will be consolidated. The two periods should be regarded as complementary and prepared for as one by the lecturer who should ensure that his audience anticipates the form of the follow-up

---

* In an experiment to find the most suitable size of tutorial group for teaching efficiency carried out under Professor T. L. Cottrell of the University of Edinburgh in 1960–1 and 1961–2, groups of 12 students obtained more favourable scores than groups of either 3 or 24.

FIG. 17. I *want* to attend this lecture: I might be interested

FIG. 18. I am *expected* to attend this lecture

period. The aim here is to direct intellectual activity towards a predetermined goal through participation.

A third arrangement relegates the lecture itself to a secondary role: it forms the recapitulation of a more comprehensive paper prepared by the lecturer and circulated to the audience at least a week or so before the meeting (*Fig.* 19). The lecture then, either restates the main features of the paper in the form of a summary or supports them with different, but closely

FIG. 19. I *must* attend this lecture because it is so important to me

related, data. In this lecture the personality of the lecturer should not intrude into the subject matter.

The duration of this form of lecture will tend to be short—about twenty minutes is often sufficient—in order to provide for a longer discussion than would otherwise be possible. The discussion is taken down and transcribed into typescript after which it is first circulated to the participants from the audience. When they have edited their contributions the paper is passed to the lecturer who corrects and edits his replies. The paper and discussion are then published. This form of lecture is suited to meetings of learned societies: it aims at publicizing, extending, qualifying and assessing the lecturer's thesis.

The three basic lecture settings are summarized in *Fig.* 20.

ORGANIZATION

The decision to provide a lecture for a large group should not be taken lightly: if such a lecture fails, it fails many people with a great deal of publicity. It should begin perhaps three months before the actual day with an expression of need from potential members of the audience or from a

decision by a committee or board. In reaching their decision, they should
be precise about the nature of the audience, the object of the lecture and its
financial implications if these are relevant. Against this data and using reliable information, the lecturer and chairman should be proposed.

From this point an organizer should take over and book the hall. He
should then arrange for a responsible person to invite the lecturer and make

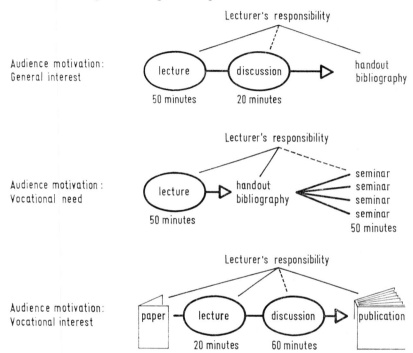

FIG. 20. The three basic lecture settings

a preliminary contact with the chairman. Many lecturers receive more
requests to lecture than they can accept and they should therefore be approached
in good time—a year in advance is not uncommon—and provided with concise but comprehensive information.

If the lecturer is a consultant he should be asked to state his fee and if he
is a member of the teaching profession he should be offered a fee of about
one two-hundredth of his annual income. (This equates one lecture to about
a day's work.) Within a school or college, a lecture of this kind should be
regarded as the equivalent of at least three classroom periods. (Inspectors,
directors and some company representatives are usually required to decline
fees.)

The lecturer will usually need to know about his audience—their background, age-range and reasons for attending—the timing of the proceedings,

the location of the hall and the route he should take to get there, the meal and hotel arrangements and, if possible, the name of his chairman. It helps some lecturers to be given a sketch plan of the hall, the positions of the electrical sockets and their type, the kind of projection and display equipment available, the nearest car park and the name of the technical assistant or caretaker responsible for the hall. The ability to find good lecturers relates fairly closely to good management.

DESIGNING A LECTURE

Every lecture to a large group must be prepared with the greatest care. This work should fall into three phases—designing the form of the lecture, composing its content and organizing its presentation: the lecturer is composer, conductor and orchestra rolled into one. Unfortunately some lecturers are satisfied if they do no more than mouth essays, turning what might have been interesting articles into, at best, unattractive and prolonged monologues.* Eminence should be no excuse for vocal vandalism.

Designing the form of a lecture involves the imagination. From time to time over days or weeks the lecture is visualized as one would visualize a play or symphony. During this phase the lecturer will decide upon his "line" and review his strategies. He should think about presenting his subject in such a way as to reveal what he feels and believes about it: in such a way as to make it *his* lecture. In this way he will give the occasion a dimension which is lacking in a printed article: it should be impossible to make a good lecture lie flat on a sheet of paper. This involvement of the lecturer is sometimes confused with the aim of the lecture but the concept of aim is too narrow and too objective to describe it. Thus we hear of "A lecture by Bragg on . . . " rather than "A lecture on . . . ."

From these thoughts the crude structure of the presentation will take shape; variations, recapitulations and illustrations will be considered in various settings until the general form becomes reasonably settled. Throughout this time the lecturer will keep his audience in mind: he will see them both as a group and as individuals: he will put himself in the place of a listener and ask how he would react. *Fig.* 21 shows some of the notes made during this period prior to a lecture on visual aids and *Fig.* 22 shows them gathered together in readiness for the preparation of the lecture itself.

PREPARATION

Although practised professionals develop individual methods, beginners should write out their lectures fairly fully. A fifty-minute lecture consists of about 5,000 words which, allowing for inevitable pauses, is a pace of about

---

* "The lecture was transferred from the lecturer's notes to the students' notebooks without passing through the mind of either." Anon.

54

110 words per minute. This means preparing about five pages of singly-spaced typescript on quarto paper.

Whilst the form of the lecture was being developed, content notes should have been made at the same time, never left to the last moment. These will include references to books and articles, to experiences, experiments and so on. When the lecture content is written, many of these ideas will be rejected since the essence of most good lectures is a structurally simple argument supporting and leading to a clearly defined thesis or point of view. Although it will contain certain facts, these should be given to bring out their implications rather than for their own sake. Even if the lecture content is itself inconclusive—unfinished research, for example—the lecturer's presentation should make this quite evident: open-ended subject matter should not result in a lecture that dies out but one that leads deliberately to a conclusion such as, "More than this we do not know and present research is sustained by the following questions: 1 . . . 2 . . . ." Highly complex arguments should be duplicated and distributed for detailed study, with the lecture as the rallying point for the main issues.

The lecture will generally consist of three or four main parts such as, for example, introduction, collection of data, the lecturer's interpretation of these data, conclusion. The purpose of each part will depend on that of the lecture itself but these should be so clearly organized that a member of the audience recalling the lecture would see it in that form.

Whilst the lecture is being prepared care should be taken to check the appropriateness of the vocabulary in which it is written. As a rough guide to their preferred mode of verbal communication, the lecturer could do worse than read the newspapers which his potential audience chooses.

He should also treat facts differently from concepts. If facts are to be remembered they must be presented in such a way as to initiate their learning. They must, of course, be presented unambiguously and this is more likely if the verbal statements are supported by visual aids. The visual and audible sensations should reach the audience simultaneously if this is possible and the fact repeated a number of times after its initial presentation. Any handout should also contain the fact in the same words and any follow-up will aim at over-learning the fact through repetition, encouragement of correct responses and immediate correction of wrong ones.

Concepts cannot be learned by rote like facts, they are built up in the mind by reorganizing facts and other established concepts. It is this process of seeking out understanding that the lecturer must initiate: he must show his group how to go about constructing the concept and indicate to them a way of evaluating their progress towards its full development if this is possible.

Thus, for example, the concept of energy might be introduced with a fact—that energy is the capacity for doing work—followed by references to different forms of energy and examples of energy changes. This might lead to slightly provocative observations such as, "I wonder if all forms of energy can be

55

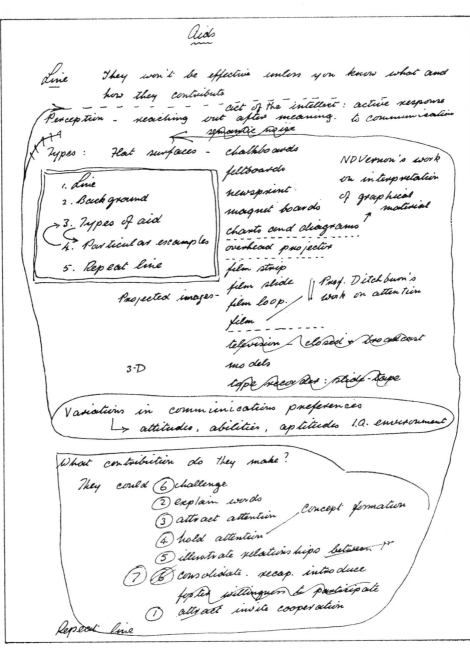

FIG. 21. Rough notes for a lecture on visual aids

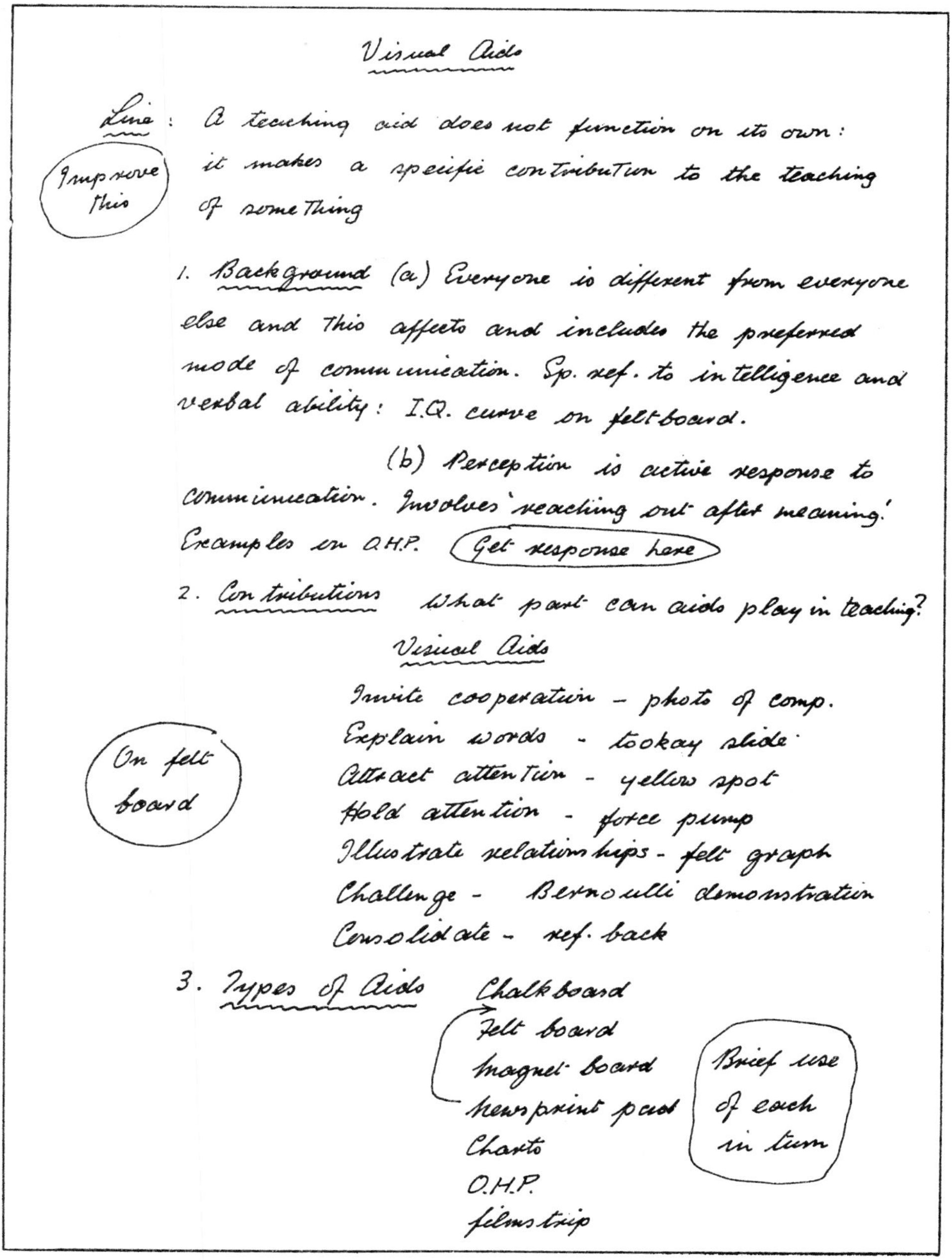

Visual Aids

Line : A teaching aid does not function on its own:
~~Improve This~~ (circled: *Improve This*) it makes a specific contribution to the teaching of some thing

1. Background (a) Everyone is different from everyone else and this affects and includes the preferred mode of communication. Sp. ref. to intelligence and verbal ability: I.Q. curve on felt-board.

     (b) Perception is active response to communication. Involves 'reaching out after meaning'. Examples on O.H.P. (circled: *Get response here*)

2. Contributions   What part can aids play in teaching?

Visual Aids

(circled: *On felt board*)

Invite cooperation — photo of comp.
Explain words — tookay slide
Attract attention — yellow spot
Hold attention — force pump
Illustrate relationships — felt graph
Challenge — Bernoulli demonstration
Consolidate — ref. back

3. Types of Aids   Chalkboard
                Felt board
                magnet board   (circled: *Brief use of each in turn*)
                newsprint pad
                Charts
                O.H.P.
                films trip

FIG. 22. Fair notes for a lecture on visual aids

traced back to energy from the sun?" or "Is the world dying a heat death?"

Facts should also be distinguished from opinions and the audience must never be left in any doubt about the validity of an observation which might be one or the other.

Of course, a lecture is an unsatisfactory source of fact-learning and, in general, should not be used for this purpose if an alternative is possible. Nevertheless facts lend an air of veracity to a presentation. Thus the statement, "This year, three hundred and twenty nine thousand, five hundred and eighteen men and women . . . —about a third of a million people . . ." has the stiff authority of accuracy which is reduced to an easy approximation suitable for retention.

VISUAL AIDS

Visual aids should be considered for the following reasons:

1. By breaking into the verbal flow of the lecture they can revive interest in the occasion itself.
2. They can focus attention on major issues and provide recapitulation or revision in a concise and stimulating form.
3. By presenting numerical data in graphical form they can emphasize their significance or bring out their meaning; and
4. They can give a measure of concreteness to abstract concepts.

The aids which are most appropriate in lectures of this kind are the overhead projector and closed circuit television. They both integrate tightly into the situation and leave control to the lecturer. Films and slides are useful but they introduce a break into the continuity and temporarily relegate the lecturer to a secondary role.

GUIDE-LINES TO PREPARATION

Introduction
1. Outline the scope of the lecture and imply (or state) the thesis.
2. Stimulate interest and centre it on the subject.
3. Show the relevance of the subject to the interests of the audience.
4. In general, make the introduction brief.

Body of the Lecture
1. Reduce this to a very few statements (two or three if possible) and prepare to lecture towards each in turn. Accentuate these main statements.
2. Support these main statements from (*a*) experience, research and so on and with (*b*) demonstrations or aids and examples.
3. Relax the pressure of information after each main statement.

4. If appropriate (*a*) present the proposition first, (*b*) follow through with objections to the proposition and expose their weakness and (*c*) give evidence for the proposition.

Conclusion
1. Retrace the argument very concisely.
2. State the thesis. Try to end in a noteworthy way.

The content should fit into a pressure-of-effort pattern as shown in *Fig.* 23.

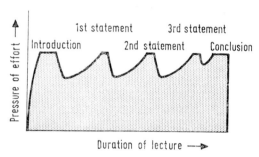

FIG. 23. Pressure of effort sequence during a lecture with three main sections

Fig. 24 shows the first section of the finished notes for the lecture on visual aids. These will probably not be used in the lecture itself but they will give the lecturer confidence. Certain critical sentences are to be learned by rote and the sequence is signposted by key words on the plan.

PRESENTATION

The test, the only valid test, of a lecturer's competence is his performance and its consequences. In this respect he is comparable with a surgeon who also depends upon extensive preparation and good teamwork. It is amoral to claim to be a lecturer on any grounds other than ability to lecture.

From the moment a lecturer begins, he must try to be as conscious of the effects of his behaviour as a surgeon is conscious of the effects of his knife. During his first few sentences he must work for co-operation. He should rise to his feet and regard his audience as one would rise to greet a friend. He will move naturally but rather more slowly than is his custom in a small room: he will speak more slowly and, if there is no microphone, tune the loudness of his voice to the remote corners of the hall. He will look at people as he speaks, not with furtive glances but with long straight looks that acknowledge the humanness of the person he sees. He will like his audience: he will not ignore any part of it.

Within a few minutes he should feel the back pressure of the group—their attitude towards him and his subject, their ability to understand, and their interest—and from this moment he can be very closely in touch with every individual except perhaps the few for whom the occasion is unsuitable. When this bond is powerful, each member of the audience associates himself with the lecturer and encourages appropriate responses in the rest of the audience. Each member too enjoys the group approval of the lecturer since he feels that he is partly responsible for the lecturer's competence.

If, on the other hand, the lecture is inadequate, each member rejects the lecturer and associates himself with the audience—the final breakdown is

VISUAL AIDS

THERE IS A widely held belief that visual aids remove the strain from learning; that in some way they premasticate what would otherwise be intellectually indigestible. Here we are often deceived by the apparent immediacy of visual perception and misled by our own communication preferences.

Learning involves

FELT   SOURCE - RECEPTION = PERCEPTION - COMPREHENSION - KNOWLEDGE

and perceptual ability depends upon a variety of factors, not least of which is intelligence. So during this talk I want first of all to glimpse the background against which visual aids are used, secondly to consider the contribution which aids make to teaching and learning and finally to make a brief survey of the aids which are available.

IQ CURVE   The intelligence spectrum
ON FELT   The relationship between intelligence and preferred mode of communication

High: Verbal, abstraction generalization, technical terms mathematical relationships.
Low: Need for thing or picture: particular cases, concrete.

In the same way ⌈ the aids we   use   and how we use them depends on intelligence.
                ⌊ Also depend on age, ability, experience, environment etc.

OHP   PERCEPTION
       Now let us see the kind of effect which occurs when we are exposed to visual information.

FIG. 24. Finished notes for a lecture on visual aids

reached when individuals become conscious of the existence of sub-groups to which they can belong when, with signals such as winks, smiles or even spoken observations, they demonstrate their allegiance to other like-minded people who have also rejected any social link with the lecturer.

Since there is no overt feedback, the lecture should be presented in such a way as to evoke active intellectual responses. This involves exploiting verbal techniques; for example, an occasional question followed, after a suitable pause, by the answer; the mid-sentence pause; sentences which end with critical words. These coax or goad or challenge the listeners to anticipate the solution. Here are two examples:

The moment of a force about a point is the product . . . (pause) . . . of the force and its perpendicular distance from the point.

60

A learner's retention is improved by making the consequence of his learning . . . (slight pause) . . . satisfying.

The same technique can be used when visual illustrations are employed. To say "I will now show you a picture of the broken muscle fibres" evokes visual confirmation whereas if the picture is shown just before the statement, "This is a picture showing broken muscle fibres" the initial response is one of interpretation which is more active than confirmation. The verbal statement constitutes reinforcement of those interpretations which were correct.

The lecturer should be natural. To prevent movements and gestures from appearing staccato he should make them deliberately and generously. If, for example, it is natural for him to count items on his fingers, he should make it obvious that he is not simply fiddling about. For the most part he should stand still and upright with his head erect. He should breathe more deeply and open his mouth more widely than usual.

Questionnaire (*See page* 62)

Please read the questions below and answer by deleting the words which are not appropriate:

1. Did you find the lecture helpful?   No/Fairly/Yes

2. Could you have learned the subject in some other way in the same time?   Better/As well/Less ably

3. The lecture period was: Too long/About right/Too short

Please give reasons for your choices in the questions below:

4. The section of the lecture which I felt to be most valuable was concerned with . . .

5. The section of the lecture which I felt to be least useful was concerned with . . .

6. The section of the lecture I enjoyed most was concerned with . . .

7. The section of the lecture I enjoyed least was concerned with . . .

8. I would rate this lecture as

    A—lucid, inspiring, absorbing

    B—clear and interesting

    C—a useful experience

    D—difficult and dull

    E—a waste of time

ASSESSMENT OF A LECTURE

To improve the standard of his presentation, a lecturer should painstakingly learn from the responses of his audience and the criticism of his peers. It is often useful to invite senior colleagues to attend and to discuss the lecture afterwards. A tape recording can be made and played back, but lecturers are warned that these are often unflattering and should be used with understanding.

The most direct and reliable guides are video-taped records which can be made during lectures on "home-ground." These should be discussed with colleagues when they are played back in order to derive the greatest value from them.

The other important source of information is the questionnaire completed by all, or a sample of the audience and, so far as they are concerned, collected by the organization rather than by the lecturer himself. The example on page 61 has been of value to the author.

GUIDE-LINES TO PRESENTATION

1. A dull, sceptical or sleepy audience needs stimulating: increase their pulse rates by making them apprehensive, anxious or amused. An audience which laughs and gradually feels a bite beneath the humour finds relaxation very difficult.

2. If they already understand some of the lecture, tell them so and explain that you are recapitulating: if the lecture is one of a series relate it to the rest.

3. Give guidance on notes, handouts or further reading.

4. Decide the extent to which the audience should be entertained, informed, instructed, encouraged, inspired.

5. Have a "line", make it known and acknowledge the existence of others.

6. Be prepared to complete the sentence, "If they have derived nothing else from my lecture, every person now understands . . . (or is able to, or wants, or, etc.)."

7. Collect information about your performance.

REFERENCES

1. KLEIN, JOSEPHINE, *Working with Groups*, London, Hutchinson, 1961.
2. UNIVERSITY GRANTS COMMITTEE, *University Teaching Methods* (The "Hale Report"), London, H.M.S.O., 1965.
3. *The Report of the Committee on Higher Education* (The "Robbins Report").
4. THE FUND FOR THE ADVANCEMENT OF EDUCATION, *Better Utilization of College Teaching Resources*, New York, 1959.
5. MOBERLEY, W., *The Crisis in the University*, London, S.C.M. Press, 1949.
6. TRUSCOTT, B., *Redbrick University*, London, Faber, 1943.

5 COMMUNICATION FOR SKILL

There is no clearly defined boundary between the ability to perform a physical skill and the ability to manipulate facts and concepts: they fuse and merge so that, for example, the skill of speaking, the ability to remember words and their meaning, and the ability to organize what is said, are inextricably synthesized. However automatically a skill may be performed, every element of it is supervised by the brain, albeit unconsciously, and the moment one of these elements is interfered with the brain takes over at the conscious level and makes greater or smaller adjustments to offset the interference. Thus a carpenter, planing wood, does so without thinking about the process until, say, he hears the metallic click of the plane iron against a nail when he consciously begins to cope appropriately with the obstruction.

There are greater or smaller elements of skill involved in almost all we do: reading, writing, talking, walking, filing metal, filing papers, expressing disapproval and holding hands in the dark, but for the purpose of this chapter we shall devote our concern to the kind of economical organization of psychomotor activities which is recognized as skill by those of us who teach and train. We shall refer to such activities as fitting and turning, typing, driving a car and tying a shoelace rather than those which do not involve the physical manipulation of tools, machines or materials, but most of what is said will be equally applicable to the skill components of more specifically intellectual activities.

The fact that the performance of some physical skills seems to involve no intellectual activity whatever tends to obscure the process which goes on inside the performer and this, in turn makes communication about the process difficult. According to John Dewey, "anything from Greek to cooking is intellectual in that it promotes thinking." To return to the carpenter planing wood, provided the interferences he meets are common to the tool and material he is using—changes in grain density, small knots and the like—the adjustments he makes to meet them are almost automatic ones: he modifies his performance as an *immediate* response to the sensory impressions he is receiving as he performs the skill. In doing this he makes no intellectual reference to experiences outside what he and the tool and the material are doing at that moment: his brain is therefore free to manipulate ideas outside the immediate performance of the skill. It may, for example, range over such questions as, "Is this grain-form suitable for the finished article?", "Does this finish call for the use of a scraper?", or he may reflect outside the task—"The scent of pitch pine reminds me of my holiday in Sweden," or he may daydream. This, then, is skill—the closed loop containing the receptors whence sensations are sent to the sensory control centre, the effectors which respond to the control and the links between them (*Fig.* 25).

The untrained consciously perform the components of a skill as connected but discrete movements controlled by the sensory channels which are appropriate to each item. The trained perform serial movements which are triggered

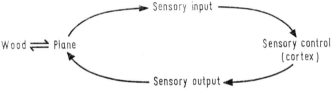

FIG. 25. The closed sensory loop of skill

off by an initial perceptual activity: this leaves sensory channels relatively free for the reception of other information. Training should be planned to effect this change in behaviour.

TRAINING

Training for skill, then, involves communicating to the learner that sequence which will enable him most effectively to become part of the closed loop and then to provide him with sufficient experience to become unconscious of the part he plays in it.

The basic raw material factors which affect this learning are those which affect all learning—age, intelligence and sensory acuity—although the effects they have may differ from those they have on academic learning. The senses involved are those of touch, vision, hearing, sound, smell and kinaesthesis: the latter sense being associated with the deep-seated nerve endings in the muscles, joints and tendons which provide information about the positions of parts of our bodies and the movements they are making. Whilst bowling at a game of cricket, for example, the kinaesthetic loop holds us on course and delivers the ball, leaving our brains free to process the visual information instant by instant and match it against the major tactical decision we made as we began the run-up: our body becomes a sort of bowling machine and our brain trims and refines the direction and spin and release angle in the light of the most recent data which it can use. The muscular movements of the run-up, themselves set up the impulses by which they are regulated. This "riding of the mind on the body" is even more evident during fencing.

THE PURPOSE OF TRAINING

Certain of the movements we make are responses which are built into us as we are formed before birth. These are the foundations upon which we build a superstructure of other acquired or conditioned responses as described in Chapter 1. Thus the innate reflexes of reaching for food and kicking for exercise develop, by a process of conditioning, to the skill of walking. As we have seen, this process which occurs because it is accompanied by sensations of satisfaction, or relief from discomfort, results in very powerful learning.

Since this conditioning process can also interfere with skill-learning or prevent it altogether, training of some kind is frequently essential to success. Thus, for example, a man who teaches himself to use a typewriter, generally begins by using two fingers only, because we are early conditioned to point with the index finger, to touch small things with it and to pick up small things with one or other index finger and thumb. For a beginner to start typing with two fingers therefore "comes naturally" and is quickly reinforced by the success which follows. Equally, he is conditioned to look at the keys—we always look at the things we touch unless we consciously persuade ourselves otherwise. With reinforcement, and after years of typing with two fingers whilst looking at the keys he becomes fairly proficient at using the typewriter. But the truly skilled typist who uses ten fingers types faster, more accurately, without looking at the keys and with less fatigue than the two-finger man will ever achieve. In such a case, the instructor must divert the student's learning *away from* the direction of natural conditioning until he becomes conditioned to the initially unnatural fingering.

Skills can be learned by a process of trial and error and, indeed, this must always be involved in skill learning to a greater or less extent. Thus in the absence of instruction, learning to drill metal with a hand drill involves turning the handle too quickly and then too slowly until what seems to be the "best" speed is learned; this can take a long time and include trials over a very wide range of turning speeds. One object of training for skill therefore, is to reduce the amplitude of the variations in the trial-and-error process. Sometimes the choice of the optimum conditions for skilled working may never be made correctly as is likely in the case of the very slow speed which should be chosen when drilling brick with a carbide-tipped drill: this is when theory must be taught to provide the substructure of understanding which underpins correct practice.

Once a skill is learned, the performer needs to be master, not only when its performance is unimpeded but also when variations or even crises occur. Thus a fully trained and skilled man can continue to perform his skill at an optimum level after, say, damaging a finger, because he knows the reasons why he performed as he did before the damage was done. He can make the best possible job of routing with a chisel when no routing tool is available because he knows the principles of routing, the cutting action of chisels and the physical characteristics of wood.

Training, then, is necessary

(*a*) to reduce the time, effort and frustration which trial-and-error learning might involve,

(*b*) to initiate the establishment of good habits from the outset and hence eliminate the need for extinguishing natural operant conditioning and then retraining,

(*c*) to provide external references which enable the skilled man to accommodate any variations in demands which the materials, his tools or his body makes on his performance.

In our changing industrial environment the last purpose of training assumes considerable importance. The nineteenth-century horologist, for example was trained when he produced his masterpiece—a concrete testimony to his competence—but his present-day counterpart may move from watch to rocket mechanisms and on to work and processes unthought of today. His skill, like the tip of the iceberg, is supported by a considerable body of technological reference and—to complete the simile—supported by the ocean of his general cultural education. The paradox of an industrial society is that the increasing exploitation of mass production and automation techniques demands a greater fragmentation of skills fitted into a wider frame of educational reference.

PREPARING TO COMMUNICATE SKILL

Certain simple and natural skills like breaking things with a hammer can be communicated very efficiently by unaided demonstration—animals learn from one another in this way. It may be that this lies behind the extent to which industrial training consisted until recently of simply watching and copying a trained person, and may support the processes which go on in some schools of art and recreational centres where students pick up skills rather than learn them in an organized way.

But most skills can be learned more efficiently if they are taught with understanding. This involves, in the first place, finding out what a fully skilled performer does, how he does it and how long he takes. In industry, the sequence of movements involved in a skilled operation can be found from its work-study specification and this can constitute a reliable basis for the training officer to work from. Otherwise, the skilled operation must be observed and broken down into its components—the more detailed this is, the more precisely the trainer will know what he is communicating. At this stage it is unwise to rely upon introspection alone because some movements become so automatically integrated into the total pattern of which they are a part, that we perform them unconsciously.

66

Thus the crude breakdown of the skill of planing the face side of a piece of wood with a smoothing plane would include observations on the following:

1. Adjusting the stop to suit wood.
2. Placing wood.
3. Picking up plane and moving to planing position.
4. Making the cutting stroke.
5. Recovery and returning to the planing position.

The actual process must now be studied more deeply in order to find out how the skilled worker achieves his results. For example, during the cutting stroke with a smoothing plane a craftsman makes subtle adjustments in his body balance and hand pressure to keep the nose of the plane pressed just hard enough on the wood for the iron to cut to a constant maximum depth but not so hard as to impede the steady forward travel of the tool. Details of these adjustments must be added to the list of what the skilled man does. In the description of planing with a smoothing plane, this column would include an analysis of the craftsman's stance, his method of holding the plane his eye movements and the points and direction in which he applies pressure.

At this stage it is useful to break down the speed at which the skill cycle is performed. It must be kept in mind, however, that the speed is considerably affected by the perception involved and that a skilled performer will considerably slow his pace when he is required to attend closely to a perceptual aspect of the skill. Thus his speed of filing will be reduced as he closely approaches a line to which he is filing. This is even more apparent in the novice: if he were told as his first exercise to practice filing an intricate profile he would make very slow progress indeed and his acquisition of the skill might be considerably retarded as a consequence of his learning a distorted balance of priorities.

The next step involves looking for any sensory demands which might be excessive. In typewriting, for example, the use of fingers other than the index fingers is unnatural and will call for special training or additional exercising, in flying an inverted aircraft the responses to the rudder are reversed and additional visual references become necessary, in piano tuning, greater than normal concentration on beat notes is called for. In the acquiring of such skills, pretraining of some kind may reduce the learning time by reducing the regression consequent upon repeated failure to perform the whole skill with the fluency for which the learner hopes.

In most such cases as these, the process consists of replacing an established "set" in a sensory channel by another. Thus in learning the skill of inverted flying we must develop a different series of responses from those which have become habitual in flying the right way up.

Since the process is one of conditioning, a simulator is sometimes an effective training machine. In filing the edge of metal, for example, the natural movements produce, not a flat surface, but a concave one and this the learner

67

readily over-corrects to produce a convex one. Before he can file to a shape, he must first master the skill of filing flat and this is learned most quickly on a filing simulator which shows a red light (say) if the file is tilted one way and a blue one if it is tilted the other. His correct filing is therefore continuously reinforced if the lights remain off and his errors are visually corrected immediately. In the bad old days, piano teachers sometimes rapped the wrists of pupils when they dropped their hands below the best playing position. This negative method was also effective but research shows that positive reinforcement provides a more permanent motivation by directing the learner's efforts towards success rather than the avoidance of failure.

The last preliminary is to discover the kinds of faults which learners make, the reasons why they make them and the actions they should take to correct them and prevent them. Here it is important to know why so-called faults should be avoided—what effect do they have on the finished product, or its sales or its reliability and so on. Trainees who know why faults should be overcome and avoided are more likely to produce faultless work than those who simply associate faults with personal criticism.

We have now pieced together the following information about the skilled performer. What does he do? How does he do it? How long does he take? What background knowledge does he use? And we have asked about the trainee. Does he need pretraining in any particular component of the skill? What faults is he likely to make?

THE TRAINING SCHEDULE

Once the training problem has been analysed in this manner the training scheme can now be prepared. The training goal should first be stated in precise and realistic terms and, as far as possible, in quantitative terms: to turn, knurl and tap a 2 BA brass terminal head using hand tools on an instrument lathe to within the limits given on the blueprint in so many minutes. It may be necessary, at this stage, to show what is meant by an acceptable finish and here too, three specimen finishes have been found valuable, one just below acceptability, one just acceptable and one very good finish: simply to say the finish must be good is meaningless.

The training goal should be followed by a note of the previous knowledge the trainee must possess. For the very first exercise for example, he will need to know about the training centre, the duration of the periods, the cloakroom facilities and so on—he will need an induction course of some kind. For subsequent sessions the needs will be more specific: to understand how to convert inches to centimetres, for example.

Now comes a decision. Should this particular skill be taught as a whole or in parts?[1] Research has produced an almost bewildering variety of answers based upon an equally bewildering variety of skills from learning poetry to pole-vaulting. However, recent work points to a pattern in these results with part methods or step-by-step methods being superior to whole methods where certain elements of the task make heavy perceptual demands. Thus the skill of measuring an angle with a sextant would be better taught step-by-step whilst that of cutting mild steel plate with a cold chisel would best be mastered by the "whole" method.

Finally the training schedule will be written and a detailed scheme prepared for each phase of the schedule. For example, using these criteria, the process of training a novice to drive a car would involve the following elements:

Introduction of the trainee to car and training procedure.

General Demonstration of the whole skill to illustrate the learning goals.

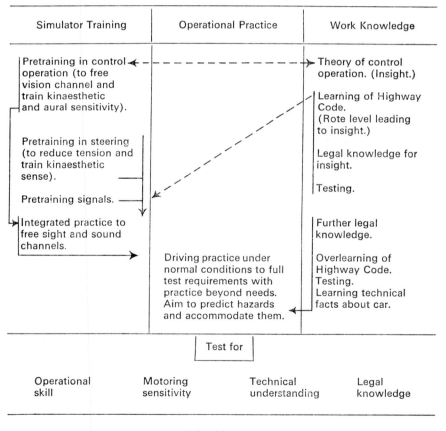

Each section of the training schedule would then be broken down into schemes.

Pretraining in Control Operation

Movements	Attention points
Both hands on wheel.	Ten to two position.
	Eyes forward on road.
Left hand to gear change lever.	
Left foot depresses	Drive free.
clutch pedal, right	
releases pressure on	Listen to engine.
accelerator.	
Ease lever to neutral, pause	Eyes on road.
slightly, push to top gear.	
Lift clutch foot gently.	

THE DEMONSTRATION

A demonstration must ultimately become "known" to the trainee and it should therefore be communicated in such a way that its sense pattern is revealed as clearly as possible. Take, for example, the skill of dancing to waltz time. The stimuli to the dancer's movements are the sound pattern and the movements of his partner. The initial demonstration should therefore communicate as much of these stimuli as possible—the "one, two, three, one, two, three . . ." can be chanted and the drum rhythm accentuated, the man dancer can be dressed in black and his partner in white. The demonstrator should spend most demonstration time with his back to the learner to give the "right-way-round" view of the skill. He should aim at communicating the interplay of the kinaesthetic, visual and aural elements until the trainee almost sees, feels and hears himself in the demonstrator's place—until he has developed an internal model of the skill.

Following a briefing to give the learner a verbal confirmation of what he already knows, perhaps a moment's pretraining on how to hold the partner and move the feet, the trainee should begin to practice.

Many skills are best learned when they are seen, not only the right way round but as they are seen through the eyes of the performer: this is the case, for example, in learning how to tie knots, adjust gauges and work on a machine lathe and it is profoundly true in learning how to manipulate things under a microscope or magnifier.

PRACTICE

This is the stage at which the training climate is tested. The trainee must know that mistakes are permitted—indeed, expected—he must be encouraged to find their causes and not dissuaded from making minor experiments in

70

order to find the best way of performing the skill within the pattern laid down by the trainer. Above all he must know how he is doing in relation to other trainees to reassure him that he is making quite normal progress and he must be aware of his success.

In some skill-learning the practice will be graded in order to stress the important perceptual elements—to highlight the figure on its ground, as it were. In tea-tasting, for example, beginners might be trained to distinguish three main different groups of tea and work from there to blends of increasing similarity.

For success in practice the learner must want to succeed, he must succeed and he must know that he has succeeded: his anxiety must be reduced: he and the instructor must have confidence in one another. In general, distributed practice consumes less learner time than massed practice provided the intervals are not overlong (an hour a morning and afternoon at most skill learning tasks would be of much the same value as five or six hours a day).

At stages during practice the trainee will make no apparent progress and, indeed, may even lose ground: he is developing new and more economical arrangements of sensory responses and sequences and this involves a slowing down of the performance itself. Such stages are called learning plateaux. When he finds he is not improving, the learner can easily regress and become disheartened and it is here that the instructor should be particularly concerned to show that this relaxation of advance is expected and necessary to further progress.

As his skill improves with practice, his ability to distinguish relevant cues improves, the amplitude of his trial-correction procedure diminishes and his movements become increasingly co-ordinated. The trainer's work is finished when the trainee's performance meets the behavioural specification laid down in the aim and when he is able to evaluate his own total achievements unaided.

This latter ability will develop if the skill is correctly taught—if trainees are given immediate feedback of the results of their practice. That this applies, not only to young trainees but also to older workers was amply demonstrated by Belbin and Shimmin (1964).[2]

TRAINING AIDS

The most important training aid in certain fields is the simulator designed to provide realistic practice with immediate feedback of results. This is desirable for operator training in a complex highly automated installation like an oil refinery, gas plant or chemical works where an operator's adjustment of one control can modify a number of interdependent factors. It is high time simulators were introduced into training schemes for workers on equipment such as printing machinery and even machine tools. Such aids, not only enable trainees to work without the anxiety of making expensive mistakes, but give them immediate knowledge of the effects of such mistakes once they are made. The cost of equipping many training establishments and technical colleges could be dramatically reduced by the development of suitable simulators.

It is essential too, to use simulators where danger to life would be involved in training under working conditions as in some phases of pilot training, and the use of safety equipment. For the greatest value, a simulator which is the sole source of experience before the trainee begins working on the real thing, must provide the whole spectrum of sensory experience and must involve the trainee so completely as to become the real thing in the trainee's mind.

Many simulators are used as a stage in the training programme when they are designed to demonstrate one aspect of the process to which the skill applies. When they are used in this way they will be designed to accentuate this aspect and to attenuate others.

To facilitate some learning, the trainee should see the skill performed as though through the eye of the performer. For this, the most suitable medium of visual communication may be a loop film (for repetitive work of up to four minutes per cycle), a film or closed circuit television where the camera can be operated beside the eye of the skilled performer. For operations with a long cycle of repetition such as instrument assembly work, aural cues may be provided by a tape recorder—the stages being initiated and checked against the verbal information provided at the depression of a foot switch. More comprehensive audio-visual cues can be provided by a video tape recorder connected to a television monitor. Always, where aids to correct sequencing and perception cueing are employed, they must give, not only the cue but some reinforcement of the correct response.

Analyse the skill.

Define the learning goal precisely in behavioural terms.

Demonstrate the whole skill with verbal guidance.

Give pretraining in unnatural or excessively demanding parts of the skill.

Provide distributed practice of whole skill as soon as possible.

Give verbal or physical guidance: encourage correct behaviour and explain reasons for changing wrong attempts.

Test when the learner is succeeding.

REFERENCES

1. SEYMOUR, W. DOUGLAS, *Industrial Skills*, London, Pitman, 1966.
2. BELBIN, E. and SHIMMIN, S., Training the Middle-aged for Inspection Work, *Occup. Psych.*, **38**, 1, 49–58, 1964.

FURTHER READING

BEVERIDGE, ANDREW, *Apprenticeship Now:* Notes on the Training of Young Entrants to Industry, 168 pp., London, Chapman & Hall, 1963.
CLEUGH, M. F., *Educating Older People*, 185 pp., London, Tavistock, 1962.
SEYMOUR, W. DOUGLAS, *Industrial Training for Manual Operators*, 203 pp., London, Pitman, 1954.
SEYMOUR, W. DOUGLAS, *Operator Training in Industry*, 52 pp., Institute of Personnel Management, 1959.

THE MEDIA

6   AUDIO COMMUNICATION

Face to face talking is more than audio communication; indeed in some face to face conversations words are of insignificant consequence compared with the information carried by other channels. This may be made obvious enough by the nonsense noises of adults talking to babies, by young couples under the influence of moonlight or politicians praising their opponents, but it is none the less true in different degrees of all conversations. Thus the overt utterance of the word *yes* may mean *no* or *go away* or *your ability to add a few simple numbers makes me wonder how you got this job*, or a thousand and one other meanings. In face to face communication the whole sensory field is of significance—the smell of a young baby, for example, the softness and warmth of its skin, the noises it makes, the sight of it and even the taste of the fingers it pokes into your mouth are all meaningful components of the whole experience. Consequently audio communication unsupported by the normal complementary sensations is an experience of a different quality from face to face communication.

First of all our need for a context in which to accommodate the sensations we receive evokes a creative response: we put a person to the voice, the person in a place and so on. The effort of doing this is apparent only when the voice has an unusual quality or says unusual things although evidence of our having created an image is usually provided, for example, by seeing a radio personality for the first time.

Secondly the effect of listening to words being said is different in quality from that of reading them. The voice of the commentator carries nuances of meaning which give another dimension to the words themselves: equally a piece of music played under one conductor has different qualities from the same piece played under another and both differ in their impact from that of reading the score. Yet these differences are carried in the words themselves (or in the music) and therefore evoke a special creative effort on the part of the listener (*Fig.* 26).

Two qualities of audio communication then, are of significance to teachers:

  (i) its power to supercharge the meanings of words and sounds, giving them a dimension which is absent in books and scores;

(ii) the demands it can make on the receivers' initiatives of imagination.

Three sources of audio communication are of interest in education and training; radio, players of recorded sound and telephones.

RADIO

Radio has an air of authority for learner-listeners: it is associated with up-to-dateness, expertness and authenticity. It can recreate the past and make it,

FIG. 26.   Listening is an active response to aural communication

in many ways, more past-in-the-present than books can; it can connect to any place and join people and places together. Psychologically, accepting the "magic" of radio dwarfs to insignificance the difficulty of spanning time and distance and frees the listeners' minds from the higher hurdles of imagination which they must go over when they read.

Radio can assist in keeping teachers up to date, provide realistic contexts for academic studies, put learners in touch with leaders and experts, provide up-to-the-minute information and bring together a variety of things, people and places.

But radio lessons can be efficient only if they are planned with the same precision and understanding as other kinds of lesson. The radio contribution should fit naturally into its context. Generally there will be a pre-listening preparatory phase leading without haste or pause to the broadcast which will lead into the follow-up and consolidation phases. The radio should, therefore, be tuned in advance and the class should be in suitable listening positions

75

when the loudspeaker is switched on. The preparatory phase should be used to motivate the students to listen critically; the teacher should adopt a participative role so that at the moment of switching on "we" are tuning to the set for information. During the broadcast the teacher should listen with his group, setting the pattern for their response by sitting in the front row, laughing when it is funny, concentrating when it is difficult, looking at the study guide when it is called for and so on. By sharing the experience with his students, not only does he reduce the psychological gulf of superiority without losing prestige, but he teaches his students how to listen. His aim here should be to guide them to discover that listening or not listening can

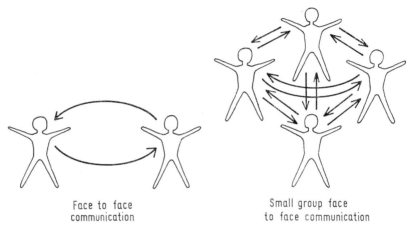

Face to face
communication

Small group face
to face communication

FIG. 27. Face to face communication

depend upon intellectual control and not on transient and irresponsible whims, that listening is the active response of the receiver of audio-communication and that the will to listen is the civilized qualification for speaking. Communication is a sharing of ideas or experiences (*Fig.* 27), and discriminatory listening to radio is a sophisticated exercise in this process (*Fig.* 28).

In general it is unwise to encourage note-taking during a broadcast as this interferes with hearing, let alone listening. It is therefore important to see that the listening period fits into an environment of purposeful activity:

1. "Here is the subject and we must listen for answers to these problems or for information in these areas or for his views on these aspects of the question" . . . and so on.
2. Listen . . .
3. "What do you think of that" or "Now let's try the problems or experiments he, or jot down notes on this before we forget" . . . and so on.

Such integrated listening requires as close an understanding between the teacher and the broadcaster as circumstances will allow: mutually planned broadcasts, study guides available to teachers sufficiently early for scheme planning and feedback of results and comments from the teachers to the broadcaster after the event. Since experience shows that teachers' comments frequently neutralize one another and are often expressions of teachers' fears or preferences or self-esteems and so on, it is highly desirable to oversee some selected broadcasts with a team of professional psychologists.

One other important quality of the radio broadcast is its transience: this can be offset with a tape recorder but it can also be exploited. It demands

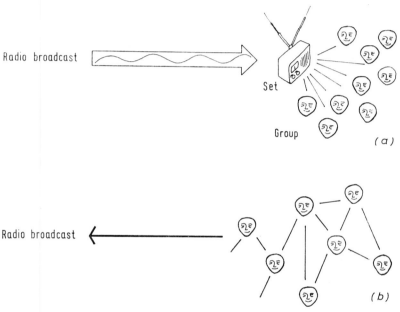

FIG. 28. (a) Listening (b) Discussion leading to reports which modify a subsequent broadcast

critical listening and, with practice, this capability can be extended by its use. Lucid and concise speaking may also be encouraged by means of a broadcast simulator: a microphone in a simple studio connected through an amplifier to a speaker in the classroom. Indeed, at Bilston College of Further Education, this technique has been extended to become a daily five minute "broadcast" of music, discussions and lecturettes to the whole college and has proved a rewarding innovation.[1]

Some Technical Notes
In order to exploit the medium of radio to its best advantage the equipment should work well and unobtrusively. Medium- and long-wave signals are as good as they can be but international agreements, by restricting the range of frequencies available to broadcasters, make it impossible for the highest

77

musical frequencies to be transmitted on these wavebands. Furthermore, since these transmissions are amplitude modulated, they are prone to interference from other broadcasts, from electrical machinery and switches. Although these shortfalls are sometimes difficult to detect they provide reasons for choosing equipment suitable for the reception of VHF-FM (very high frequency—frequency modulated) signals, which carry the full spectrum of musical frequencies and are almost immune to interference.

A centrally placed receiver is ideal provided the installation is professionally designed to allow classroom speakers to be switched on and off without

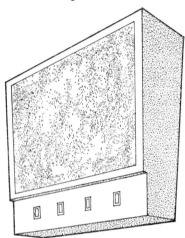

FIG. 29. Classroom loudspeaker

changing the reception characteristics elsewhere. With this system, good quality receiving equipment can be installed, connected permanently to a properly designed aerial and never moved. Such an arrangement is particularly recommended for large schools because it combines economy with quality, and for tower blocks where the movement and storage of portable equipment present an obvious problem. Of course, only one programme can be distributed at a time unless more than one receiver is fitted but, in general, this is rarely a problem.

With this arrangement, the speakers are mounted in the fronts of the classrooms—one eight-inch speaker in a suitably constructed container is ample for each average room of, say, 5,000 cubic feet. However, it must be remembered that students of all ages will be tempted to switch it on and, not for this reason alone, the classroom controls should be proof against misuse. One of the best arrangements consists of a row of four switches beneath the speaker. Any one of them connects the speaker at volumes increasing from left to right. Switching lower volume switches makes no difference to the output already given by a higher volume one (*Fig.* 29). This pattern can be seen in colleges of the Inner London Education Authority.

Training establishments are probably best served by an AM/FM set of sturdy construction incorporating a firmly mounted speaker of, say 7 in. × 3½ in. Such an instrument would weigh about 10 lb. For the most natural conditions, loudspeakers should always face the listeners unless they are specially arranged to reflect from a wall.

GRAMOPHONE RECORDS

Gramophone records of music are, for the most part, audio works of art. They are played on record players to enable students to hear what music sounds like or what voices sound like and consequently their value lies in the extent to which they provide an accurate rendering of the original sound. This imposes certain disciplines on those who buy and use them.

The attitude of caring for records can be learned unwittingly and, because records are culturally important, this unwitting learning should be deliberately fostered. No record should ever be out of its sleeve unless it is being played on a turntable, and it should be handled with a combination of technical precision and affection.

A record is first made on magnetic tape using instruments and materials of impeccable quality. This tape is then played back into a kind of record player in reverse which causes a chisel cutter on its arm to cut a groove in a black lacquer-coated copper disc. As the disc rotates, the cutter moves inwards from the edge to the centre and at the same time the audio variations on the tape make it vibrate, the result being a wavy spiral. Unmodified in any way, the loud low-frequency passages would produce lateral movements considerably larger than those caused by loud high-frequency passages with certain intolerable consequences. The playback pick-up arm would tend to jump the grooves unless it were very heavy and the distance between grooves would have to be so large that the playing time for each record would be very short. To eliminate these drawbacks the low frequencies are attenuated and the high ones amplified so as to produce the most acceptably uniform waveform over the whole of the audio spectrum. The pattern of this adjustment is called the recording characteristic and, whilst it is unnecessary to know the rather complicated nature of these systems it must be appreciated that the original sound is most nearly approached if the first stages of the receiving amplifier exactly reverse the compression that has been impressed on the recording. High quality amplifiers do this.

After the groove has been cut, the disc is coated with graphite to make its surface an electrical conductor and it is then copper-plated. The copper is peeled off, strengthened, and used to make a negative from which a final positive is produced. The positive—the mother—is then used to make negative chromium-plated stamping discs which, fitted in heated presses, are used to stamp out the polymerized vinyl chloride records. A record then, is produced by a team of artists, scientists, technicians and craftsmen, and is

79

generally a product of extremely high quality. It may have surface blisters or little pits in it and these can be seen in oblique lighting with a magnifier: it may be warped as can be found by placing the record on a glass plate. Records with these rare imperfections should be exchanged.

CARE OF RECORDS

Since records are now so precisely made and so smoothly polished, there is far less background noise due to imperfections than heard in an actual concert. But this standard of production can be exploited only if the records themselves are kept clean.[2] Since the force with which a modern stylus presses into the record groove is so very small, it rides over the dust and grease, pressing them together to make a new groove bottom and, as it does so, it adds unwanted hisses and clicks to the recording.

Consequently records should be handled without touching the recorded area and kept in their sleeves when they are not in use. Each new record should be lightly wiped by holding a slightly damp lintless cloth over it as it turns on the turntable; it should never be wiped across the grooves. This treatment reduces the likelihood of its becoming electrostatically charged and of attracting dry dust. The same process, or one like it, should be repeated each time the record is played, keeping in mind that the greatest care is needed with records used under the lightest stylus pressures. Naturally, the turntable itself should be free from dust and its lid should be closed except whilst the disc is being moved.

Records should be stored vertically, loosely together on shelves as in a record shop.[3] They should not be retained once their playing quality has appreciably deteriorated.

A turntable of such a weight and driven by such a motor (generally a four-pole constant-velocity motor rated at about 15 watts) that it is not slowed down during loud passages and maintains a uniform running speed throughout each rotation is called a transcription unit. Only turntables of this quality match modern recordings although cheap turntables of very good quality are available. A worn idler wheel in a turntable drive can cause a periodic variation in speed which is audible as a periodic pitch fluctuation: this is known as "wow." Worn drives can cause a similar but quicker pulsation called "flutter." The electrical arrangements in the motor can cause hum and the sound of the vibration of the moving parts coming via the pick-up is called rumble. If these defects arise in transcription units they can be remedied by servicing.

It is possible to obtain auto-change equipment of very high quality, but the small advantage it offers is no compensation for the risk of damaging records. Indeed, lifting and placing the pick-up calls for such care that an arm lifter is desirable when parts of a recording are to be selected for playing (*Fig.* 30).

The critical device, so far as record wear is concerned, is the pick-up (*Fig.* 31). It is estimated by Decca that the "pick-up in most of today's radiograms and modest record reproducers destroys at the very first playing

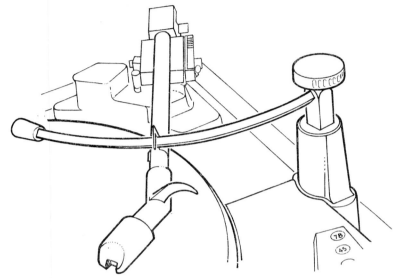

FIG. 30. One type of pick-up arm lifter

up to thirty per cent of the information so painstakingly captured on record by the manufacturers." This wear is due to the enormous pressure exerted by the stylus on the groove wall (*Fig.* 32), the tremendous accelerations which

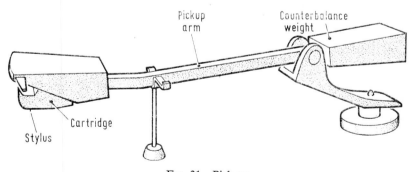

FIG. 31. Pick-up

the stylus makes to follow the groove, the tip mass—the mass of the moving part—of the stylus, and the stiffness of the stylus support. If the pressure is reduced by reducing the downward force of the stylus on the record it will ride over grooves and not move with them and this limits the possible playing weight reduction. As a rough working rule it is unwise to allow this

81

force to exceed five grams and to check it periodically with a pick-up balance. The tip mass and the freedom of stylus movement—its compliance—depend on the type of pick-up chosen and constitute the most critical factors in record wear.

The record-player pick-up consists essentially of an arm fitted with a stylus which tracks in the record groove, and a so-called cartridge in which the mechanical vibrations of the stylus are changed into electric currents. Naturally, a stereo pick-up will contain a "double acting" cartridge capable of separating the sounds received in the two recording microphones and its stylus will be fine enough to suit the more complex stereo groove; its tip

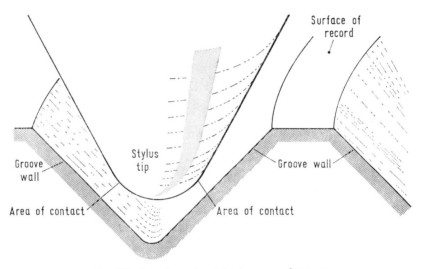

FIG. 32. Location of a stylus in a record groove

radius will not be greater than 0·0007 in. Stereo records can be played with mono cartridges and under certain conditions and with some pick-ups will not be damaged by them. Details should be obtained from the manufacturers.

A sapphire stylus will probably give about fifteen hours playing life, after which the facets rubbed on to its sides become so deep that there is a possibility of the tip of the stylus running in the bottom of the record groove. Under these conditions the rate of record wear has been measured by Philips to be six times normal. A diamond may play for anything from six hundred hours to thousands of hours before it needs replacement and whilst it is wise to check sapphires every six weeks by viewing them under a low power miscroscope in oblique lighting, diamond checks need be made only every six months (*Fig.* 33).

For classroom equipment the compromise between quality, wear and cost is probably best met by using one of the cheaper transcription pick-up arms

82

with a diamond stylus and setting the tracking weight on the stylus to that given by the maker or to about four to five grams if there is a wide choice. This setting is higher than professionals use, but it should prevent the stylus from groove jumping even when there is a certain amount of vibration of the

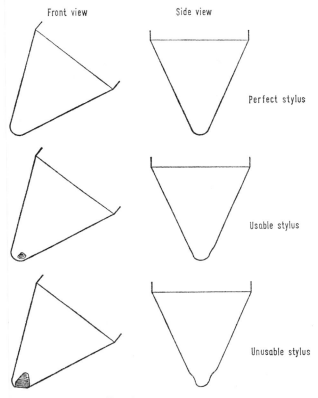

Front view   Side view

Perfect stylus

Usable stylus

Unusable stylus

FIG. 33. Stylus wear

turntable under classroom conditions, provided, of course, the turntable is absolutely level. It is most important to check this.

The stylus movements are converted into electrical variations in the cartridge and these must be amplified in order to become sufficiently powerful to drive loudspeakers.

Amplifiers for record players are also suitable for amplifying the output from microphones, tape recorders and radio tuners but if they are to give the best performance of which they are capable they should match electrically the equipment with which they are used. Thus the output from a magnetic pick-up might be 20 mV at 33 kΩ whereas from ceramic pick-ups and also from crystal ones it might be 60 mV at 100 kΩ. The amplifier should therefore be matched for the particular type of cartridge in the player or it should be provided with at least three sets of input terminals for high output magnetic pick-ups, low output (high quality) magnetic pick-ups and crystal pick-ups. In general, good amplifiers will also be provided with inputs suitable for tape heads, tape reproducers, radio tuners, high sensitivity microphones and low sensitivity microphones. Such an instrument offers versatility with quality.

The complete record playing system is shown in *Fig.* 34 and this is often contained in a single cabinet. If, however, the record player, the amplifiers and the loudspeaker can be housed separately, certain advantages follow. The most obvious one is that the loudspeaker enclosure can be designed

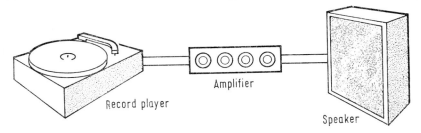

Amplifier

Record player

Speaker

Fɪɢ. 34. Record playing system

solely to produce the most realistic sound and it can be positioned to give the best performance.

The corresponding complete stereo record playing system is shown in *Fig.* 35. A stereo cartridge converts the two-plane vibrations of the stylus into two separate sets of electrical variations corresponding to sounds recorded from two spaced microphones. These separate signals are separately amplified and converted back to sound again in two loud speakers. The controls on the amplifier are identical with those on a mono amplifier except that a *balance* dial is added to enable the loudnesses of the two speakers to be correctly adjusted.

Stereo sound is most successful with small groups and with the speakers spaced about eight feet apart. Then the best audio results will probably be experienced in the area shown in *Fig.* 36. However, this depends upon the acoustics of the room and, in the end, will be found by experimenting.

When using stereo equipment it is essential to connect the speaker leads the right way round. To check this, put the speakers about a foot apart and facing each other, play a stereophonic record—a vocal one is best—and listen to it with the head between the speakers. If the leads are correctly connected the singer will appear to be in front.

TAPE RECORDERS

Recording tape is made from a strip of acetate, P.V.C., tri-acetate or polyester coated with a varnish containing magnetic iron oxide. If a magnet is

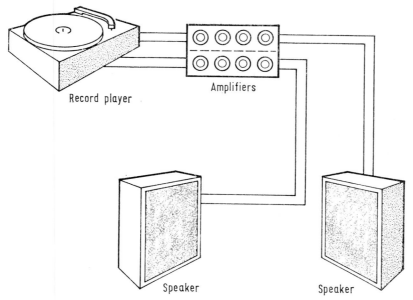

FIG. 35. Stereo record playing system

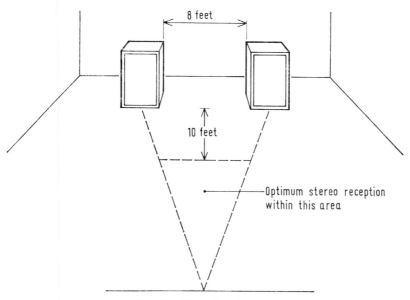

FIG. 36. Stereo hearing area

moved across it, the tape becomes magnetized and if, now, the tape is pulled past a coil of wire, it will make a tiny current flow around the coil. It is on this principle that tape recorders work.

Recordings are made on tape by passing the varying electric currents produced from a microphone or radio through an electromagnet and at the same time moving the tape at a constant speed over its poles. This imprints corresponding magnetic variations on the tape. When the tape is run at the same speed between the poles of another electromagnet with its winding connected to an amplifier, the magnetic variations cause corresponding

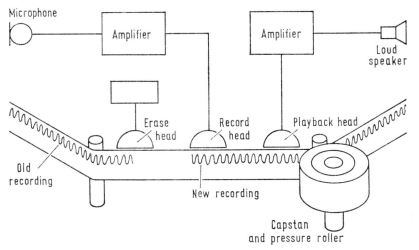

FIG. 37. Tape recorder

electric variations which when amplified are converted back to sound in a loudspeaker (*Fig.* 37).

In most recorders, the same electromagnet is used both for recording and for playing back from the tape. There is, however, another separate electromagnet over which the tape passes before it gets to the record/playback head. This is the erase head and when the recorder is switched to RECORD a high frequency current oscillates in its coils. This stirs up the magnetized iron particles so that, as they move away from it, they become less and less magnetized in any particular direction. The demagnetized tape then passes across the poles of the recording head which imprints its electric signals on to it as magnetic ones.

When the recorder is set to PLAYBACK the erase head is disconnected from the circuit.

Recording tape is a quarter of an inch wide and in two-track machines the top tenth of an inch width passes across the heads. When the tape is turned over the other edge can be used. On a four-track recorder, the heads are

86

made to record and play back from either the top quarter width or the next-to-bottom quarter width of the tape when the spool is one way up: when reversed the remaining quarters can be used (*Fig.* 38).

Two-track stereo recorders have two heads working on the top and bottom halves of the tape whilst the heads on four-track stereo recorders are exactly like their mono counterparts: they differ in feeding double amplifying systems.

Recorders may operate at one or a number of tape speeds, the most usual ones being $7\frac{1}{2}$, $3\frac{3}{4}$ and $1\frac{7}{8}$ inches per second whilst the slower speed of $\frac{15}{16}$ and the higher speeds of 15 and 30 inches per second are also standard. The faster

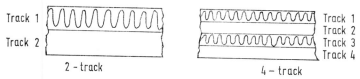

FIG. 38.   Recording tape used in 2-track and 4-track recorders

speeds give better quality reproduction, particularly of higher frequencies and therefore the sound produced from them seems more brilliant. They also make editing by cutting easier. The slower speeds are generally perfectly adequate for speech and, of course, use less tape.

Tapes also vary in thickness—standard play is thickest at two-thousandths of an inch, then long play, double play and triple play. A 7-in. spool of double play tape gives about $8\frac{1}{2}$ hours' playing time at $\frac{15}{16}$ inch per second on each track whilst a 7-in. standard tape plays for about half an hour at $7\frac{1}{2}$ inches per second on each track. The thinner the tape, in general, the more it will stretch in use and the more likely it becomes that loud passages will transfer ghost images to adjacent loops.

As with record players, a good external speaker will give very much better reproduction than an internal one which of necessity must be small in size and fitted into a less satisfactory enclosure. The standard symbols used for connecting sockets on tape recorders are shown in *Fig.* 39.

The heads on a tape recorder correspond in function with the pick-up on a record player. If they become dusty or dirty they should be cleaned around with a stiffish brush and the cleaning finished with a lintless cloth which should be pulled through the path taken by the tape. The capstan which pulls the tape through the heads and its pressure roller should also be checked periodically and cleaned if necessary since pieces of oxide or tape may build up on the drive and cause "wow." Check too that the tape runs true. If the speed of the recorder seems to vary even after cleaning, the machine needs servicing.

Never bring any metal near the recorder head or it may become magnetized, and, as a result, a steady hiss will be heard in the speaker during playback. If this happens, the head must be demagnetized by holding a "head defluxer" against it, switching on, and moving it away slowly to a distance of about a foot and then switching off. Any dealer will do this very cheaply.

Care of Tapes

Whilst tapes appear to withstand quite rough handling they are, in fact, vulnerable to physical damage, particularly on their edges. The great enemy of tapes, as with tape recorders, is dust so they should be out of their cases only so long as they are on the recorder for use.

Sometimes with thin tapes, a faint copy of adjacent layers becomes transferred during storage. This can usually be avoided by recording at moderate volume and by keeping the tapes in boxes in a reasonably dry cool atmosphere.

FIG. 39. Standard symbols for audio equipment

Very small battery driven transistorized tape recorders using tape only 0·15 in. wide and permanently contained in plastic cartridges are ideal for portability. They give a total playing time of 2 × 30 or 2 × 45 minutes and play at $1\frac{7}{8}$ in. per second, and although their size precludes the possibility of high quality reproduction, they can be connected to and played back through a normal amplifying system as well as through their own tiny internal speaker. Then the reproduction is very good.

Editing Tape

There are three methods of editing tape: the first is to copy the tape to be edited on to a second tape making the additions and alterations by starting and stopping the machines to suit. This, at first, seems to be both simple and economical but the work itself is very tiresome and the results are often highly unsatisfactory. The second is simply to erase what is not required and then to fill in the blanks with suitable infilling material. This too, has its drawbacks: it is difficult to match the infilling both in quality of recording and in content, and fitting back parts of sentences is extremely difficult in practice. Perhaps the most straightforward application of this technique is to fade a constant background into the gaps—music rising in loudness between snatches of conversation, for instance.

Generally the most satisfactory method is to cut the tape and join it together again in the required sequence. Incidentally, this does not waste tape since the joined tape can be used again and again, just like an uncut one. Before a tape is spliced, the position of the cut must be marked with a yellow or white wax-based pencil; remember that the sound recording at any instant is at the recording head. To avoid damage to the head the mark is made at a guide pillar and the distance from there to the head allowed for (*Fig.* 40). The tape is cut with non-magnetic scissors or, better still, on a jointing block. For very precise joins the cut should be made at right-angles across the tape and for a physically more satisfactory one at 45°.

Two splicing techniques are available, one using jointing tape and the other jointing solution. The adhesive tape is simply stuck to the non-coated faces of the two ends to be joined and then trimmed. The solution method takes a little longer but gives a permanent join. First the solution is brushed

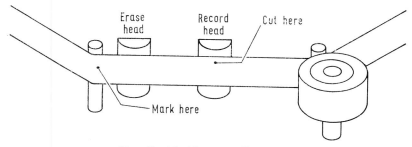

FIG. 40. Marking a tape for editing

on the coated side of one end of tape to cover a strip of about three-sixteenths of an inch. This dissolves the coating which is then wiped off with a lintless cloth. More solvent is applied to the cleaned face and the other tape end pressed on to this area for about half a minute.

Tapes should be indexed as they are completed, by marking the tape with wax pencil or by marking the supply spool or by reference to the mechanical tape position counter. The index should be kept inside the tape box and a corresponding index card filed in the library under a code number. Individual items on the tape should be separately indexed in the same way as books. Thus, under the library subject index one might find, "WOMEN: Social position. (The) Place of women. Discussion with Dutch students at Gaulsheim, 1967. Tape 82." The card for tape 82 would give the position of the discussion on the tape and there would be a copy of the index inside the tape box.

LIVING WITH MICROPHONES

If it's a microphone—don't blow it.

There are three main types of microphones; crystal, moving coil and ribbon, their quality, price and delicacy increasing in that order. The crystal microphone is light in weight, cheap in price, gives a high output and matches the high impedance input on an amplifier or tape recorder. It picks up sound equally from every side, and is therefore said to have a circular polar diagram. It makes a good lapel microphone.

Moving coil microphones vary in quality but generally give better results than crystal ones: they have a lower output. Most of them are omnidirectional like crystal microphones to low frequencies and unidirectional to high ones, but some have a cardioid polar field, that is sounds are picked up equally along a heart-shaped curve as shown in *Fig.* 41. All moving coil microphones

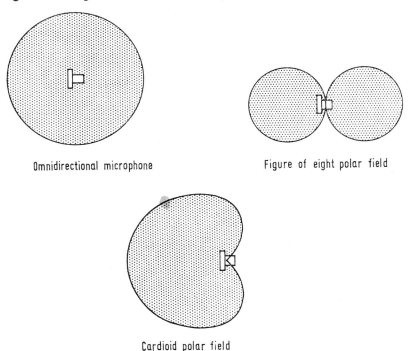

Omnidirectional microphone   Figure of eight polar field

Cardioid polar field

FIG. 41. Polar fields of microphones

match the low impedance inputs of amplifiers unless they are fitted with a built-in transformer to convert them to high-impedance instruments.

Ribbon microphones, which give excellent quality reproduction have a figure-of-eight polar field (*Fig.* 41) and a low impedance: they really are fragile both electrically and mechanically and should be covered with a thin plastic bag if they are used in draughty conditions.

Microphones with a circular diagram do give slightly different qualities depending on the direction in which they point. Sound from in front is sharper and from behind is more mellow, so even with such an instrument, its angle and position relative to the sound it is receiving are of consequence.

90

Cardioid and figure of eight instruments are ideal for most live recording, first in order to select sounds that are wanted and secondly to enable basic effects, such as the movement of sounds to be easily contrived.

Whatever instrument is chosen it must match the recorder or amplifier—high impedance microphones (high Z of high Ω) must connect to similarly marked sockets. And the leads from high impedance microphones must be short ones whilst low impedance instruments can be fitted with leads of up to fifty yards long without encountering any problem.

The quality of the sound recorded from a microphone will also depend upon its position in the room, the type of room and the way it is furnished. An unfurnished room without carpet or curtains, with large glass windows, will give a lively echoing sound, a soft furnished room will give a dead one. Distortion by reverberation may be due to sound bouncing from the surface of a polished table and this can be reduced by covering the table with a felt cloth. Opening windows reduces reverberation.

Only by experimenting can the best effects be obtained, but some general guide-lines may help:

Never speak too closely to a microphone: a foot is about the least distance for good reproduction. If the room noise forces you to speak with the microphone close to the mouth, speak across its surface to reduce the intensity of the explosive consonants such as p.

Speaking into a corner usually produces a crisp effect whilst speaking away from it mellows the result.

Discussion groups should form a circle around an omnidirectional microphone and a semicircle in front of a cardioid one.

Lecturers who move about are best served with a halter microphone or a radio microphone which transmits from its little box to a separate receiver connected to the amplifying equipment.

For drama, talks and so on in which simulated radio programmes are produced, draw on the floor the actual polar diagram around the microphone showing the areas in which speech can be heard clearly, satisfactorily, with difficulty, and not at all.

LANGUAGE LABORATORIES

Tape recorders and microphones constitute the electronic hardware of language laboratories. Each student works independently, often at his own pace, listening to a language programme and responding to it by recording through a microphone. He can go over work as often as he wishes, he can call for help from the teacher sitting at his console. The teacher can, unobtrusively, listen to an student, give him guidance or record passages for him on his own recorder.

91

Some laboratories give emphasis to learning only by hearing whilst others make use of visual guides and cues. Whilst the relative merits of different kinds of programmes are difficult to assess it seems that the visually aided ones are more useful for younger learners. There is no doubt that the ability to converse usefully in a foreign language is learned far more quickly through language laboratory programmes and that with adults, spaced practice does not seem to result in a more efficient learning rate. Courses of three weeks' or more uninterrupted language learning in a laboratory have proved highly successful. The criteria by which such programmes should be developed and assessed are discussed in the chapter on programmed learning. A radio

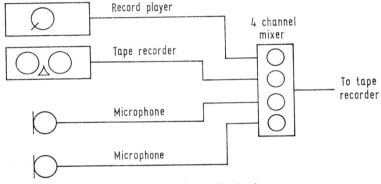

FIG. 42. A radio studio simulator

studio simulator for student exercises, can be made with the aid of a mixer as shown in *Fig.* 42.

TELEPHONES

The method of using a telephone well can and should be taught to certain employees. This involves three interrelated phases: the techniques of handling telephones and switchboards taught as a skill, the manner of speaking for comprehension and reliability with particular reference to the importance of feedback, and the development of those personal qualities through which good relationships can be established and maintained.

Techniques are best taught through graded practice with simulators. Reliability exercises should involve the use of test material so that the learner is constantly aware of the progress he is making. The development of a good telephone personality may be guided by tape recording telephone conversations made by students during role playing exercises and playing them back for small groups to discuss.

92

REFERENCES

1. CRICKMORE, LEON, An Experiment in Broadcasting, *The Vocational Aspect* (Spring 1967), Vol. 19, No. 42, pp. 50–8.
2. WATTS, CECIL, E., *A Guide to the Better Care of your LP and Stereo Records*, Darby House, Sunbury-on-Thames.
3. CURRALL, HENRY F. J. (Ed.), *Gramophone Record Libraries: Their Organization and Practice*, 183 pp., London, Crosby Lockwood, 1963.

FURTHER READING

NISBET, ALEC, *The Technique of the Sound Studio*, Focal Press.
SPRING, P., *Tape Recorders Performance Analysis and Servicing Techniques*, Focal Press, 1967, 207 pp.

7 VISUAL AIDS AND THEIR USE

This chapter divides into three sections, the first devoted to a brief survey of the contributions which aids can make to teaching and learning, the second to a review of the types of aid which are available and the third to methods of making and using those aids which a teacher could prepare for himself.

Basically, teaching and training are intended to evoke in the learner's mind patterns of ideas similar to those which exist in the teacher's mind, and whatever intermediate stages are involved, the learner must piece together these patterns from sensations of sound, sight, taste, smell and feeling. Because of an innate belief that words spoken by the teacher are the most important communication link between teacher and taught, we refer to other sources as though they were ancillary and call them aids. Yet there are countless occasions when spoken words are aids and the major source of communication is a picture or a movement or a smile of encouragement.

Unfortunately, it is easy to be deceived by the apparent immediacy of visual perception when the response, "I see," may be taken as meaning, "I understand," and for reasons that have been discussed, this is more likely to happen in public lectures than in small group teaching. Errors of judgement of this kind will most likely be avoided if the functions of aids are analysed: knowing the contributions they can make is basic to using them well.

Learning is most likely to be efficient in a happy harmonious atmosphere. But in such an atmosphere people do most things more efficiently: they digest their food better, relax more completely and sleep more soundly. Consequently, whilst first-class social relationships between everyone in a group provide an essential background to the greatest likelihood of successful learning, the focal point of effort must be provided by the learning itself.

During a lesson, students learn some things by making a deliberate effort to do so. In this way they assimilate, to various degrees of understanding, some of the information which is taught. These efforts begin with the learner making a conscious decision that the subject matter is of interest to him—even if the interest is primarily directed to avoiding some unpleasant consequences of not knowing.

Some learning appears just to happen and no conscious effort is involved. This unwitting learning often has a powerful influence on the learner and constitutes an important element in propaganda, religion and tradition. Not only in schools, but also homes, factories and offices, its effects are reflected in attitudes towards neatness, accuracy, safety, punctuality and behaviour as well as in actual subject knowledge, skill and experience.

And we have seen that learning at either the conscious level or the unconscious level is affected by the environment in which it takes place. This is true too of what we see. The environment affects not only what we are able to see but also what we believe we do see. The same close-up of a face on a screen will be a sad face or a happy face, a relaxed face or a worried one depending upon the story or even the music which goes with it.

The teacher should provide a kind of subject environment by beginning each element of subject matter with a general idea of the whole of the matter he intends to teach—in everyday terms, he must give his students a "general idea of what it is all about" or, in the case of a skill, let them "get the hang of it." This will soften their initial apprehension and help to overcome the resistance to learning which it engenders. Often, the best way of doing this is to show a film or a series of pictures, to use a model or to demonstrate with apparatus: words alone often make impossibly heavy demands on creative and imaginative abilities at this stage.

This first overlook in a kind of progressive synthesis is more in keeping with the laws of perception than the logical process of building the whole in small linear steps. In "getting to know" naturally, we enlarge our knowledge by changing it qualitatively, by subjecting it to analysis from different and increasingly critical points of view.

Once students have acquired a general impression of the whole, its details can be taught until they are understood. This is usually easier for the learner if his attention is first directed to the simple aspects of the subject and then guided to increasingly complex ones, from particular examples to general ones and from concrete aspects to abstract ones.

But in all this, difficulty, of itself, is not a deterrent; indeed it constitutes an essential attraction and since most knowledge becomes permanent only if it is overlearned, difficulty must often be injected into a subject in order to hold the learner's interest. For example, the multiplication tables become permanently known after they have been used over and over again to solve a wide variety of problems and not through learning them only sufficiently to repeat them.

Finally, because a desire for social approval spurs the will to work, learners need to assess their progress and to compare it with that of others. To do this they must give expression to what they have learned and to derive a full measure of incentive from this expression, their efforts should attract recognition.

USING AIDS EFFECTIVELY

This professional knowledge of the way we learn forms the matrix in which ideas about aids are best able to crystallize: it leads to decision about how they should be used.

Roughly speaking we can divide aids into two groups: those which amplify the effectiveness of the mechanics of transmitting and receiving sensations, and those which contribute to the teaching-learning process. In the first category are microphones, projectors, TV sets and so on; in the second such equipment as diagrams, models and gramophone records.

Irrespective of its function or effectiveness, an aid will often earn ancillary dividends by evoking the co-operation of the group. In using an aid, a teacher implies that he is aware of the existence of difficulty—he confesses, as it were, to a sense of sympathy for his learners. Also, shown something—particularly if it has been made especially for them—students regard themselves as persons of greater consequence because they have been thought about outside the actual lesson time. This is equally true of a worker's response to his instructor or a selling agent's attitude to a demonstrator from the company he serves. Indeed, even if the aid is only partly effective in illustrating the subject matter, it may make students want to learn successfully in order to show their appreciation of the teacher's interest in them. The value which is derived from this reaction is difficult to assess, but when good social relationships are enhanced by the teaching method itself, the resultant improvement in efficiency is focused on learning and not directed to relaxation.

Of course an aid can be used to attract the student's attention, but its capacity for doing so can be two-edged. For example, strike a match and an entire group will look and wonder. They will go on looking for a while as they await an explanation. But if none is given, or if what follows seems to be an anticlimax, a reaction sets in and the students will direct their attention elsewhere—talk to one another, begin writing or reading—in order to redress the slight which made their eagerness seem foolish. By all means let the aid become a focal point of attention: strike the match deliberately, watch it inquisitively and keep perfectly quiet. But when every mind is intent on the flame, use that moment of attention to teach something worthwhile and teach it forcefully.

Aids can supplement verbal explanations. One of the most delightful examples of this is Prokofiev's "Peter and the Wolf": the story is made vibrantly alive by the music.

Fig. 43(*a*) is an aid which supplements a description. *Fig.* 43(*b*) is a visual which tells its own message. *Fig.* 44 is more fundamental since it provides an explanation of the meanings of two unusual words. If a critical word in a sentence is not understood, or is misunderstood, not only does the sentence become useless but the learner's belief in his prospect of success is weakened. Care in this respect is doubly necessary when a technical man is lecturing to a lay audience.

An aid may be used to hold students' attention whilst a lesson is being taught. To this end, a moving aid will generally hold attention for longer than a static one. The basic thermodynamics of heat engines, for example, might be taught with reference to a slowly pulsating home-made hot-air engine. Then, since this will be the focal point of attention, the lesson should be taught as an explanation and extension of the engine; it would be wasteful for the teacher to attempt to compete with it for his students' interest. This ability to become, in such circumstances, an unobtrusive commentator needs to be cultivated to the pitch of the students' believing that they have learned from the aid alone. Not only will the learning then be easier but much more

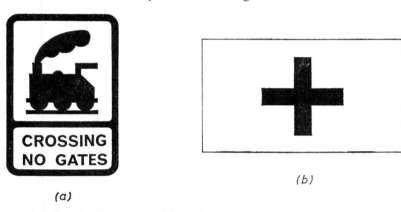

(a)

(b)

FIG. 43. Visual messages: *(a)* supplements words, and *(b)* replaces words

satisfying. Magnetic boards designed to illustrate mechanisms or rules can be employed in this way with considerable success, provided the teacher works in the knowledge that the aid is the focus, and he is a mere extension of it.

It is relevant to emphasize here that "learning by doing" can sometimes be less efficient than "learning by observing," for insights into problems are cultivated through mental rather than physical activity. Galperin, the distinguished Soviet psychologist goes so far as to conclude that "practical activity tends to inhibit thinking," and that "children learn better by observing a concrete demonstration and verbally anticipating the teacher's steps."[1] When students work in pairs in laboratories, those who organize, control and observe the experiments, often develop a deeper insight into the subject than their partners who actually perform them. Equally, role-playing sessions are often of more value to the observers than to the participants. It is interesting in this connexion that the Progressives were misunderstood by their supporters in that activity was taken to mean *physical* movement whereas the actual concept as seen by Dewey was much wider.

More often than not, aids which are designed primarily to illustrate relationships take the form of graphs (*Fig.* 45(*a*)) symbols or simple

97

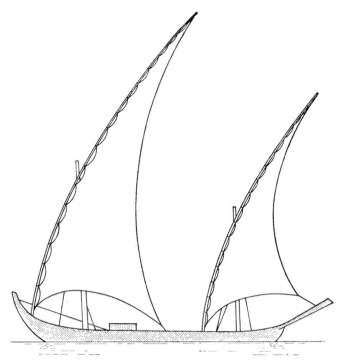

FIG. 44. The bows of the Nile Gyassa are bluff to prevent their sticking in the river mud. A visual that "explains" words

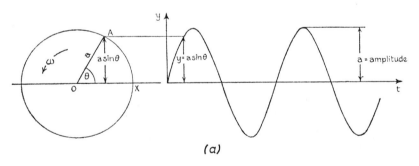

(a)

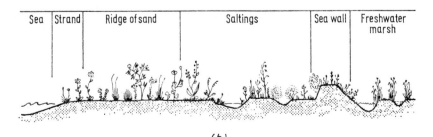

(b)

FIG. 45. (a) Information as a graph, and (b) stylized graphical information

alternatives to graphs (*Fig.* 45(*b*)). Here the relationship itself should be dominant and uncluttered: verbal explanations are better support data than written labels.

Learning causal relationships of a scientific kind however, involves a great deal more than attending to graphs. Such relationships are not a series of steps like a Euclidian proof, but a structure within a structure. Research points here to the value of learners' elaborating their own interpretations before the final structure of the relationship is developed: this is the basis of Nuffield science in which the "aids" are apparatus and models of appropriate kinds. Conventional aids would be used in the summarizing phases.

In mathematics aids can give a measure of concreteness to the subject. A large triangle, for example, can be scored as shown in *Fig.* 46 and then

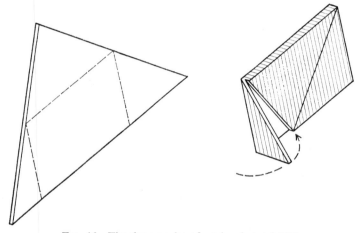

FIG. 46. The three angles of a triangle total 180°

folded to show that the sum of its three angles is 180°. The actual presentation is, of course, most effective if the card is coloured on only one side. This mode of presentation of mathematics may be employed to create a general belief in the subject matter to which the rigour of deductive mathematics will come as a rational conclusion.

The illustration of some relationships poses interesting problems. In making a history chart, for example, should the time scale be linear or logarithmic? In other words, does 10,000 years "look" a hundred times as long as 100 years or only twice as long? To decide, it is essential to draw it out and look at it.

Another function of an aid is to present information in such a way as to challenge students to learn. A coloured plate in a cookery book could do this provided the standard it set did not seem impossibly high and the context in which the food was displayed did not appear socially foreign to the student. Aids which challenge learners do so, as a rule, either because they offer a

99

reasonable opportunity of success—the crossword puzzle—or because they appear as a reasonably balanced battle of wits between the learner and the teacher. An example of the two types combined is often found in the film or tape-recorded introduction to a role-playing session. This offers a dual challenge: one from the characters portrayed on the record ("We've got ourselves in a mess and you can't get us out of it!") and the second from the public nature of the solution. Consequently, the more "real" the problem appears to be, the more likely is the challenge to be stimulating.

The type of aid which requires a student to complete an incomplete drawing or sentence, to identify flash cards, aircraft recognition silhouettes and so on,

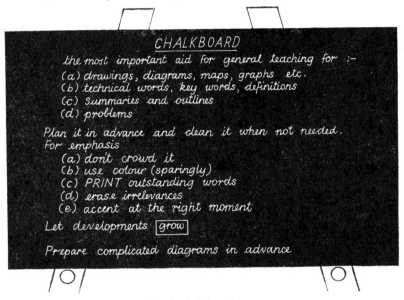

FIG. 47. A chalkboard summary

can be the basis of a challenge if the students associate the teacher closely with the exercise. Here, the attitude to encourage is comparable with that of a tennis coach stretching the capabilities of his pupil in a game. The students should want to "beat" the teacher, should enjoy some success, and should believe that the teacher is also enjoying the evidence of their growing abilities.

Some challenges can be more subtle than this. Things on display which can be compared, one with the other, are often more attractive—and consequently more useful—to students because they feel drawn to find similarities and to evelute them. In this category we have "before" and "after" examples, which range from samples showing the effects of processing to illustrations of sequences in the development of a major project.

Finally aids may be used to consolidate what has been learned, or to generalize a group of ideas. Such aids will be used after the subject matter

100

has been learned in order to bring it together and give it form and also to remind learners of the progress they have made.

Some films and filmstrips are valuable in this capacity; the feltboard can be extremely useful, but for many teaching occasions there is nothing to compare with a summary of a lesson which has been developed on a flat surface, step by step, as the lesson has progressed. This, because of its immediate association with the learning, is known to be completely relevant. *Fig.* 47 shows a summary which has been built up on a chalkboard during a lesson: *Fig.* 48 shows a summary in the form of diagrams on a feltboard. To summarize:

---

1. Aids can—Invite co-operation
           Attract attention
           Supplement verbal information
           Hold attention
           Illustrate relationships
           Challenge
           Consolidate

2. Through unwitting learning they can help to change or strengthen attitudes, and contribute to the development of high standards of safety, loyalty and personal conduct.

3. The effective use of aids begins with understanding their potentialities and expecting no more from them than they are intended to contribute.

TYPES OF AID

Chalkboards

The chalkboard is the most common aid in general teaching. Conventionally, white (or yellow) chalk is used on a black (or green) surface, but dark blue or purple chalks on primrose coloured etched glass, plastic or canvas surfaces are attractive alternatives.

For effective board work it is often useful to have one board on which the lesson summary can be developed and another for such illustrations, explanations and so on, as are needed for the current teaching. One obvious group of board subjects includes drawings, diagrams, maps and graphs. These are usually best drawn as their structures are explained so that students learn as they see. Consequently they should generally be simple even to the point of becoming block schematic diagrams. Complex details are usually far better presented as duplicated handouts for close study following a general treatment on the chalkboard or feltboard. A typical pair of such presentations is shown in *Fig.* 49.

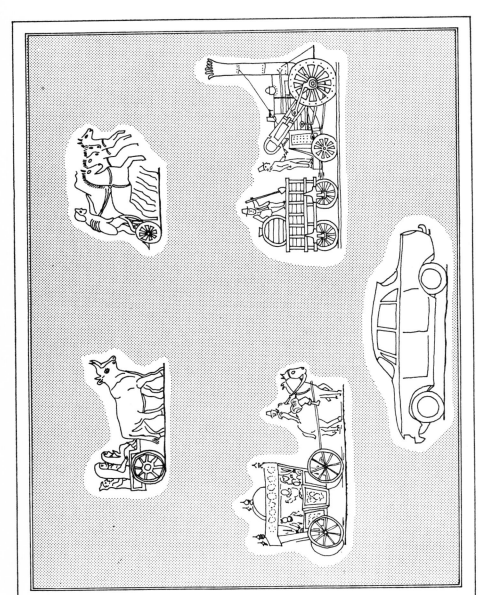

Fɪɢ. 48. A feltboard summary of a talk on the history of vehicles

Where a complicated drawing must be made on a chalkboard it is wisest to prepare it before the lesson begins and then almost erase it. The teacher can see the faint outline but the students cannot. This precaution ensures that the finished diagram will fit the board and be a reasonable shape. Of course, if there is no advantage to be gained from "building up" the diagram,

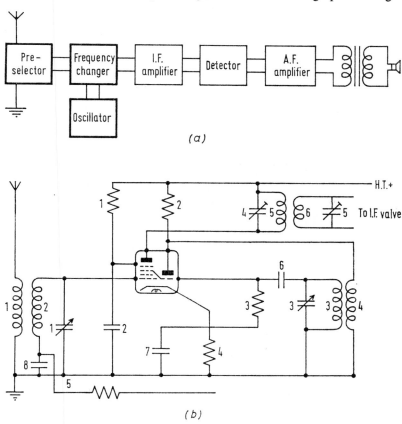

Fig. 49. Teaching diagram (a) and the corresponding duplicated handout (b)

there is no point in erasing it and redrawing it unless it is to be used late in the lesson.

Technical words, key words and definitions are given extra force if they are written on the board as they are used and then, unless they form part of a summary, erased. This gives definiteness to the presentation and is an implied invitation to the students to write notes.

Problems and their solutions should remain on view for only as long as the students are using them: their transience gives emphasis to the dynamics of the learning and, if a summary is being developed, gives that the major prominence. At the end of the lesson, the latter should be the focus for the teacher's recapitulation.

It is difficult to generalize over so versatile an aid but, as a rule, a chalkboard should be planned in advance and cleaned when it is not in use. For emphasis it should be uncrowded, colour may be used sparingly, outstanding words can be printed in capital letters or boxed in, and key words can be spoken and written simultaneously. Abstract ideas can be represented by

FIG. 50. Abstract ideas can be represented by shapes

shapes (*Fig.* 50), people by stick figures (*Fig.* 51), quantities by size (*Fig.* 52) and so on.

Improved versions of the chalkboard include white and coloured plastic boards with writing surfaces suitable for felt pens containing water-based ink: this can be cleaned off with a damp cloth or paper tissue. Stained surfaces can be cleaned with a very dilute bleach.

Blocks of newsprint make useful alternatives to chalkboards. Wax crayons and felt pens are not messy like chalk, but with such materials diagrams must be right the first time they are drawn as they cannot be erased. To this end it is wise to pre-prepare them in 2H pencil which can easily be seen by the teacher but not by the class. Well used in appropriate circumstances—each sheet being torn off as it is finished with and thrown in a waste bin or turned over to be used again for revision—it gives quite an impressive suggestion of the teacher's mastery of his visual aid medium.

Feltboard, Plastigraph

Surfaces on to which shapes, diagrams and captions can be fixed, simply by placing them in position, are special alternatives to the chalkboard. They

FIG. 51. — people by stick figures

can be used with very large groups of people because the prepared material can be made suitably bold. With these devices the display of visual data and the recording of summaries is a matter of a moment and does not interfere with the flow of discourse: it can, quite dramatically, accentuate the essential

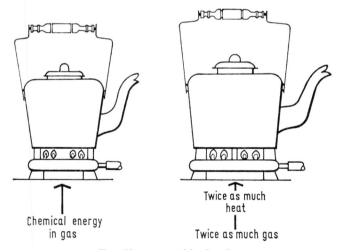

Chemical energy
in gas

Twice as much
heat

Twice as much gas

FIG. 52 — quantities by size

steps in a lecture sequence. Of course, the fact of using pre-prepared material reduces both the versatility of this group of aids, as compared with the chalk-board, and also the intimacy of the presentation.

Plastigraph comes in very bright colours, can be cut into well-defined shapes, and has a strong visual appeal, but folded pieces have to be peeled apart and dust can interfere with adhesion. The soft pliability of felt, on the other hand, makes the mechanics of using this medium quite unobtrusive.

Magnetic Boards

These consist of sheets of iron or tinplate—often painted so that they will also serve as chalkboards—on to which shapes, backed with magnets, will adhere (*Fig.* 53). They are particularly useful for showing the effect of moving

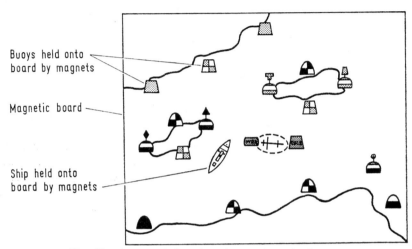

Buoys held onto board by magnets

Magnetic board

Ship held onto board by magnets

FIG. 53. A magnetic board used to teach navigation

shapes to different positions; the stages in the cycle of movement of a mechanism, traffic problems, work-study and economics problems. They can be used with the same dramatic effect as feltboards, but are really better employed where sustained observations of a series of manoeuvres, or a cycle of movements is necessary. Iron coated with a near-white plastic surface, will serve as a magnet board, a projection screen and a writing surface and can be particularly useful in preparing animation for film making.

Photographs

The chief value of a photograph derives from its air of authenticity: in the viewer's mind there is no immediate reason for its being "untrue," and any distortions will be foreshortenings of perspective which are accepted as a reasonable challenge to his ability to translate two dimensions into three. For the most part, photographs should be studied individually and without haste, and learners should know precisely why they are studying them. One technique is to use waiting time during practical sessions for this purpose, another is to display them in the coffee lounge, as these occasions offer good opportunities for informal discussion.

106

Photographs, however, generally carry far more information than corresponding line drawings and consequently they are more suitable for intelligent learners whilst line drawings are often more suitable for the below average learner.

Photographs taken at stages during the development of a project, or on a field trip, can facilitate follow-up study: if this consists of a lecture, the pictures would probably be displayed from an episcope.

Good photographs appropriate to a course of study, which have been enlarged to, say about 2 ft × 1 ft 6 in., mounted in a deep frame and changed periodically never fail to attract intelligent interest. Smaller photographs, for example those which have been cut from periodicals, should be mounted on stiff cards of uniform size as this facilitates storage and turns the scrap of paper into a workmanlike instrument.

Of special value are Polaroid photographs of learners performing skills, or of stages in the course of an experiment. These "frozen movements" studied immediately after the photograph is taken can reinforce or correct with considerable force.

Charts and Diagrams

These fall into two main categories: those to be used as lesson illustrations and those for display over a period of some days or longer. The former should contain only as much visual information as is necessary to illustrate the teacher's words and the latter should be of sufficient interest to attract attention, and carry enough detail to warrant inspection and contemplation. The former supplement teaching and consequently will be complete only when they are used by a teacher: the latter must not only tell a whole story, but should contain some detail in order to justify the attention they claim. This, of course, does not apply to charts used to create atmosphere or orientate attitudes, which, since they are designed to promote unwitting learning, should be acceptably obtrusive, well defined, and framed in such a way as to become an integral part of the visual structure. Among the most successful examples of this type of display are the London Passenger Transport Board posters. On the other hand there are posters, for example, which are simply stuck up on walls in factories. Because of their content and mode of display they are seen, psychologically, as things apart from their immediate environment and consequently make only a minor impact.

Display pictures which are intended to teach must do three things: attract attention, offer difficulty in an acceptable form and present information in a fashion that evokes critical consideration. One of the simplest examples of such pictures are those which show something before and after an event so that the viewer will compare, and in comparing, will learn. Presented as a three-dimensional display, pictures attract more sustained effort than when they are flat mounted. This can be carried to the lengths illustrated in *Fig.* 54. See Plate 1.

107

Fig. 54. Examples of three-dimensional chart displays

Other devices are useful. Framing in a hole torn in a newspaper, illuminating a picture behind a small peephole, mounting pictures on a pole and so on. These may be called gimmicks but those illustrations which are so displayed as to cause viewers to make even the slightest physical effort to see them and even the slightest mental effort to adjust to their mode, sequence, angle or style of presentation, so far as the author's experiments show, are always

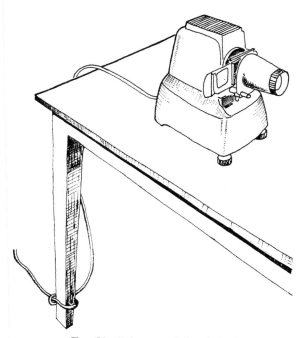

FIG. 55.   Take care of electric leads

studied more successfully than those which call for no preliminary effort beyond that of looking.

Projected Pictures
Before using projectors, teachers should take some basic precautions to ensure an elegant performance:

(*a*) See that the electric lead is safely connected: if it is pulled, it should break at a socket but not move the instrument (*Fig.* 55).

(*b*) Focus the projector on the screen. Remember that if the axis of the beam is not at right-angles to the screen the image will be a trapezium and not a rectangle. Check the screen brightness from the widest viewing angle: this should not be greater than about 30° from the axis.

109

(*c*) Check the seating and the lighting: remember—halve the distance from the projector to the screen and the image will be smaller but four times as bright.

(*d*) To prepare a film that will already have been previewed, check the sound and run the film through to the title, prior to the lesson. When the time comes to project, switch on the sound and wait for the amplifier to warm up (the speaker will begin to hum), switch on the motor and, as the titling appears on the screen, signal for the room lights to be dimmed. Dimming should take six seconds if it is to be as unobtrusive as possible.

Slides
Standard slides are $3\frac{1}{4}$ in. square and, for most training purposes, are obsolete.

Substandard slides are 2 in. square. They can be bought already prepared or they can be made photographically. Photographic slides have a greater tonal range than prints and as a consequence projected pictures can be truly beautiful. With the help of slides, lectures in geography, architecture, natural history and so on, can be made occasions of aesthetic delight as well as lucid instruction.

Modern projectors are so efficient that slides can be used without blacking out and, with a proper choice of lens and screen, the projector can be placed almost anywhere in the room (*Fig.* 56).

Projectors fitted with slide magazines can be focused and operated by remote control: this relieves the lecturer of talking from the projector or relying on an assistant. They can be operated too by silent impulses from a tape recorder. A set of slides supported by a commentary prepared and recorded by the teacher makes a stimulating component of a lesson and constitutes an astringent and valuable exercise for the teacher.

Filmstrips are simply a sequence of transparencies on 35-mm film, and are used in the same fashion as slides. There is a very wide selection available commercially, both in black-and-white and in colour.

Most strips consist of some 20 to 40 frames, each frame being 18 mm × 24 mm called single frame size. Two other sizes are made, 24 mm × 24 mm (1 in. × 1 in.) or square frame, and 36 mm × 24 mm or double frame. Most filmstrip projectors are equipped with masks to enable frames of any of these sizes to be shown effectively.

Commercially produced filmstrips are sold with sets of notes prepared for the teacher. These should be studied before the strip is used and not read during the lesson. If a teacher reads notes his presentation lacks the first-hand spontaneity which enlivens teaching and the class receive the impression that he is not familiar with the subject.

110

Microscope slides are a special form of transparency, and are projected from an instrument called a micro-projector.

Opaque pictures can be screened with an opaque projector or episcope. The most modern instruments of this type will project copies of up to 10 in. square, accommodate books and give adequate images in a room which,

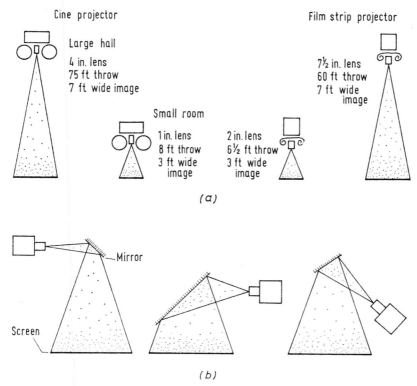

FIG. 56. (*a*) Siting of projectors should be planned for before the building is constructed. Full use should be made of back projection (*b*)

while not well lit, is not blacked out. The older opaque projectors can be used only in blacked-out rooms.

The technique of using this instrument is similar to that of using charts. The room should not be darkened until the moment the picture is to be shown, and lighted up immediately afterwards. Attention may be drawn to those aspects of the picture which *should* be observed by using a pointer or by standing at the screen and pointing.

Overhead Projectors
Because it offers a wide scope for invention as well as providing a basic service of everyday utility, the overhead projector is considered by many

111

responsible teachers to be the most versatile and valuable aid at present available. It is a clean, often superior, substitute for the chalkboard; it gives clear images in well-lit classrooms; it can project prepared transparencies of many kinds; it can show moving diagrams and models and project many experiments as they are performed. Yet, and this is an important quality, its contribution is almost exclusively an expression of the teacher—it enables him to do something differently, or something more, or perhaps

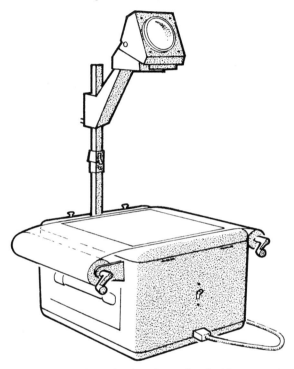

Fig. 57. One type of overhead projector fitted with an acetate roll

something better than he could without it—but he completely controls the content, the sequence and the equipment.

The instrument consists of a box with a large glass window—usually ten inches square—in its lid (*Fig.* 57). Light passing upwards through the window can be focused on a screen where it makes a picture of the order of 5 ft to 9 ft square. In use it stands on a table at a distance of about 9 ft from the screen but, of course, this distance can be adjusted widely. Table 1 gives a typical range of image sizes.

Projector lenses of shorter focal length are fitted to some instruments. These give, for instance, 84-in.-square images at a distance of 8 ft. Some instruments can be fitted with a wide range of attachments for the projection of slides and filmstrips and to facilitate the projection of demonstrations as they are performed. Some weigh about 30 lb and, although it is possible to carry them from room to room, they are best left in position and protected with a cloth or plastic cover when they are not in use. The smallest instruments weigh only about 14 lb and can be carried around very easily indeed. Some again are made to fold into box-like shapes and are fitted with carrying handles like suitcases.

There are three types of projector: one in which light from the projection lamp is reflected out of the light box and into the focusing head by a large curved mirror, another with a special lens (called a Fresnel lens) just beneath

TABLE 1

Projection distance in feet	Image of 10 in. × 10 in. transparency in inches
6	48 × 48
8	64 × 64
10	80 × 80
12	96 × 96
14	112 × 112

the glass window of the light box, and the third with a Fresnel mirror set on a $1\frac{1}{2}$-in. thick baseplate and the lamp in the projector head (*Fig.* 58).

The lightweight instruments with Fresnel lenses are fitted with very small quartz-iodine lamps which are generally rated at 400 W, 120 V. These must *not* be touched with fingers (until the lamp is burned out) and if they are handled by accident should be cleaned with methylated spirit.

In the ordinary way projectors need no special technical attention. Depending on their use, however, they need periodic cleaning with a mild solution of soap and water after which they must be thoroughly dried with a lint-free cloth. On no account should water get into any electrical components. The fan bearings need a single drop of oil about twice a year put on with a small water-colour brush.

When a Fresnel type instrument is adjusted to give a very large picture, the image it produces may have blue corners to it. This indicates that its lamp is too close to the Fresnel condenser lens and—if desirable—it can be lowered by tightening the screws holding the lamp support. When adjusted to give a small picture, the image may have brown corners indicating that the lamp is too far away from the condenser, an imperfection which can be corrected by raising the lamp support. For everyday work these adjustments

113

are unnecessary: indeed it is usually quickest simply to adjust the screen distance to produce the best image.

Since an overhead projector is most useful when it stands between about two feet and three feet above the floor, its light beam is usually inclined upwards. In some instruments the inclination is altered by adjusting the tilt of the deflecting mirror (*Fig.* 59(*a*)). The advantage of this method is that the top of the projector is always horizontal—an important requirement

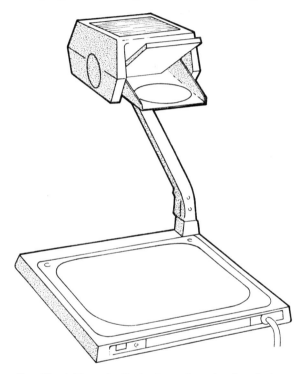

Fɪɢ. 58. A Fresnel-reflector type of overhead projector

for some demonstrations. In a few projectors the whole instrument is tilted (*Fig.* 59(*b*)).

All types of overhead projector can be used for much the same purpose as chalkboards. On many of them a roll of acetate film, 10 in. wide by 50 ft long is fitted to one side of the instrument and unrolls across the window (on which it lies flat) to another roller on the opposite side. As the teacher writes on the film with a wax-based pencil, or with a suitable pen and ink, so the image of his writing appears on the screen.

If he turns one of the rollers, the image moves across and off the screen and more writing surface is brought into position above the window. Some users—but by no means all—find this attachment very useful.

114

Pre-drawn diagrams can be projected when they are needed, and outlines completed as they are explained. The sub-headings of a lecture can be prepared in advance, leaving spaces for further notes (a useful technique for nervous beginners), and work can be recapitulated by returning the roll to its starting position and running over the notes again. If uncompleted transparencies are used they can be slid beneath the acetate roll and the finishing lines drawn in on the foil. In this way, for example, an outline map

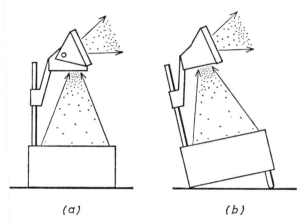

(a)   (b)

FIG. 59. Adjusting the beam elevation of an overhead projector

may be "completed" during a lesson without marking on the map itself. This is then available for further use.

Sheets of acetate film can serve the same purpose as rectangular chalkboards. Once filled with illustrations or words, they may either be cleaned or replaced by a fresh sheet. Special Cellophane sheets are available on which one can write with almost any instrument including ball-point pens. These are very cheap and especially suitable for students to use. It is advisable to fix the sheets in position with small pieces of self-adhesive tape in order to prevent them from moving or bending (*Fig.* 60).

As a substitute for the conventional board, the overhead projector has certain advantages. It is clean and can be used in situations where chalk dust would be out of place—in kitchens, metrology laboratories, instrument workshops and fashion shows, for example. It can make working with a small group more intimate and writing for groups of two hundred effortless. It eliminates the exhausting business of cleaning a large board and makes possible the retention and revision of much material. It can be used almost anywhere.

Wax-based pencil and non-etching ink can be removed with a cloth damped with ink solvent obtainable from the ink suppliers, or with methylated spirit: water-based ink marks are removed with a water-damped cloth.

115

Films

Films differ from the other projected aids in that, whilst a film is showing, it takes over the teacher's role completely. We do not see the projector since it is behind us: we simply see the pictures on the screen and hear the sounds that go with them. If the room is dark, the spectator becomes unaware of his immediate neighbours and so intense can be his attention that real identification can result in the spontaneous liberation of emotional expression. This is not possible, for example, with television where the viewing environment is visually present and the viewer can be seen by other people. Here he controls expressions of his emotions. Again with TV the set that "constructs"

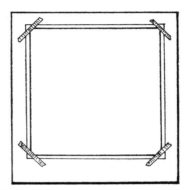

Fig. 60. Fixing an acetate square to an overhead projector

the images is there with the picture, and this too affects the degree to which identification is possible.

Since a film takes over the teacher's role whilst it is showing and can have control over viewers emotions it must be of sufficient merit to justify its solo performance, and this, in turn, means that it must be pre-viewed, pre-set, if possible, and carefully introduced. Except when it is used, either to consolidate what has already been learned, or to orientate attitudes, it should generally be shown twice. The first showing, which gives an idea of its content and sequence, should be followed by a discussion, or teaching, during which the students become clearly informed of what they can learn from the film. When they are ready for it and know precisely what they want from it, they should see it again.

It should be remembered that natural messages are received at a pace that fits in with every other associated experience whereas cinematograph messages obey laws which lie outside our everyday visual experience. Through them we see things from many angles and happening at unreal speeds of sequencing; indeed distortion is inevitable and in the hands of a skilled director is frequently exploited to enrich our appreciation of reality.

However, viewers who become bored or tired by film viewing may do so because they find the pace of presentation excessive—a fact which is frequently overlooked when teaching and training films are shown. In this case, the fact of showing a film twice will not, of itself, improve the quality of learning and another method of teaching is called for.

Film projectors should be maintained in good condition and carefully used, for neglect may harm, not only the instrument, but also the films. It is particularly important to keep the gate and gate track clean, and anyone who intends to use films would be well advised to seek expert guidance on the

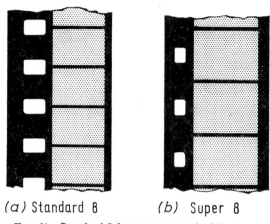

(a) Standard 8   *(b)* Super 8

FIG. 61. Standard-8 format compared with super-8

care and maintenance of projectors and on professional standards of projection.

Loop films are especially valuable and can be used by anyone however untechnical he may be. They can be integrated very closely into a lesson presentation and they can also be used for private study. Silent ones are invaluable for illustrating what the teacher is saying as he says it and, his verbal commentary can fit the level of learning of the class and, indeed, change each time the film repeats itself.

Loop films are lengths of 8-mm film with their two ends joined together so that they will show over and over again if the projector is left running. The film is made in two forms, both of which are 8 mm wide with sprocket holes along one edge. Standard-8 frames are a little larger than 4 mm wide and 3 mm deep (*Fig.* 61(*a*)) while super-8 film has smaller sprocket holes and carries transparencies about 5 mm wide and 4 mm deep making a picture area of about fifty per cent more than standard-8 (*Fig.* 61(*b*)). Loop films and loop-film projectors are available in both formats and newcomers should therefore stock super-8 equipment since standard-8 is obsolescent. Another format called single-8 is also available for normal projection but not for loop films.

Loop films are sealed in a plastic container which is shaped as shown in *Fig.* 62. The film itself is wound over a disc inside the flat cylindrical section of the cassette marked *a* in the diagram, and one loop passes between guides around the separate path marked *b*. The front flat face of *b* contains two rectangular apertures, one of them a narrow slot exposing about four sprocket holes on the side of the film. When the film is running, a claw engages with one of these exposed holes and flicks the film forward one frame at a time at the rate of 16 to 18 frames per second (f.p.s.). The other aperture—the gate—is the size of a single frame. Between each forward shift, light from the projector lamp is directed through the gate and consequently through one frame of the film to produce its image on a screen. During the very brief time that this frame is being replaced by the next, a rotating paddle shuts off the light so that every second, 16 separate still pictures are projected in sequence on to the screen, each for about $\frac{1}{32}$ of a second: the eye cannot distinguish them individually and consequently sees a "moving" picture.

Since the film runs in a self-contained circuit, the projector is smaller and simpler than the conventional cine instrument. One type, for example, fits into a case of about 9 in. long, 5 in. wide and 6 in. high (Plate 2 top). A slot in the back of the instrument takes the cassetted film which is pushed into place by gentle pressure. The "works" inside the projector include a motor drive for the film, the usual lamp and optics and a fan to keep the instrument and film cool.

When it is used with an opaque screen the room needs darkening: at 10 ft from the screen the picture width from a "standard" lens is 28 in. It can, however, be used with a translucent screen, when a small image of, say, 8 in. across will be clear in daylight.

A popular arrangement combines the projector and translucent screen with a back-projection mirror (Plate 2 bottom left). The screen is 15 in. wide and gives a clearly defined image in a classroom of normal size without completely blacking out. It is easily portable. Plate 2 (bottom right) shows a similar self-contained projector and screen.

Loop-film projector screens should be sited as close to the group as possible since they can be viewed comfortably from a few feet.

Similarly valuable are E.P. (Easy Projection) 8-mm cassettes. These take 15 m, 30 m, 60 m or 120 m of standard unlooped 8-mm film and are designed to fit into cartridge-type projectors. As the cassette is inserted into the projector, notches on it set the projection speed at either 18 or 24 frames per second. At the same time, the film is threaded and the projector switched on automatically. Conventionally reeled film can also be shown by first clipping it into the cassette: after showing, it is simply rewound on to its reel, unclipped and removed.

Closed Circuit Television

Closed circuit television is the obvious tool for teachers to use where health hazards, or location difficulties make direct observation difficult or impossible.

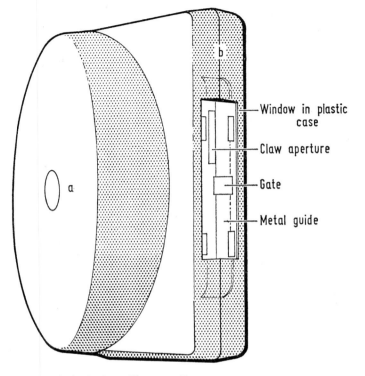

Window in plastic case

Claw aperture

Gate

Metal guide

(a) the loop film cassette

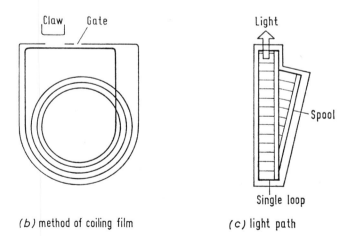

(b) method of coiling film

(c) light path

FIG. 62.   A loop film cassette

Its potential value is considerable and consequently it is dealt with separately in Chapter 8.

Models

These are the closest alternatives to real things and often more suitable for teaching purposes. Since they attract considerable interest and invite close attention, they should be sufficiently robust to withstand handling. In general, they should be left on view for long enough to satisfy the students' needs and then be returned to store.

Screens

There are two types of projection screen: the opaque type from which images are reflected (e.g. cinema screens) and translucent screens through which light is transmitted (rather like television screens).

The position and size of screen suitable for lengthy viewing sessions can be determined by physiological factors. The resolving power of a normal healthy eye—its ability to distinguish detail—is about 1' subtended angle. Consequently it is possible to see complete letters easily if they subtend about 5' and since the angle subtended by a letter decreases with the distance from which it is viewed, it must subtend 5' from a seat in the back row.

But since, many students clearly need glasses, it is unwise to cater for normal vision and a realistic angle would be 12'. If we reckon on a screen wide enough to take forty-eight characters, its width will therefore have to be about one-sixth of the distance between the screen and the outside seats in the back row.

If the seats in the front row are so close to the screen that it subtends an angle of more than 30° at the eye, it will not be possible to scan the screen by using only the eye muscles and this will cause neck-ache. The minimum distance from the observer to the screen to avoid this is two screen widths. Thus, although it is possible to see an image on a matt white screen from almost any angle, it is possible to do so in complete comfort within a segment of 30° on either side of the normal to the screen and bounded by two arcs drawn at $2w$ and $6w$ from the centre of the screen (where w is the screen width) (*Fig.* 63). Normally, screens for the overhead projector will be larger proportionately since illustrations projected from an overhead projector are rarely viewed continuously for more than a minute or so.

Glass beaded screens and some other plastic screens reflect most of the light incident on them within a total angle of 60° and therefore, provided a screen is to be used only in conditions of maximum comfort, the glass beaded type (and others with the same kind of characteristic) are the most efficient ones. For more technical details it is necessary to consult such works as B.S. 1401:1961 and papers issued by such organizations as Kodak Ltd.

On a vertical screen a tilted beam of light produces an image like *Fig.* 64 because the distance from the lens to the top edge of the screen is greater than the distance to its bottom edge. This so-called "keystone" distortion is of particular consequence with overhead projectors. Very often—despite the shape distortion and the varying sharpness of focus—this is no great disadvantage. But there are times when a uniformly sharp, undistorted image

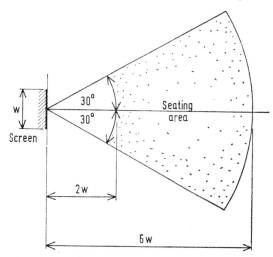

FIG. 63. Area for comfortable viewing of an opaque screen of width *w*

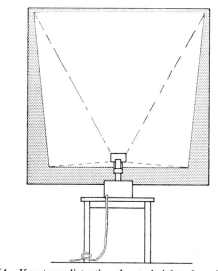

FIG. 64. Keystone distortion due to height of vertical screen

is necessary. Then the axis of the light beam must be normal to the screen (i.e. it must make a right-angle with the screen surface whether it is viewed in elevation or in plan). Portable tilting screens made for this purpose are

121

available. Alternatively, roller screens may be mounted on the ceiling away from a wall and their lower ends fixed to the wall (*Fig.* 65). A very good arrangement is to have a correctly angled permanent and solidly constructed screen surface built into the room.

Where normal viewing is difficult, the screen can be situated at one side of the room as in *Fig.* 66(*a*). For tutorial and seminar work where the teacher sits and discusses with a small group, a portable overhead projector on a very low (coffee) table with the group arranged as in *Fig.* 66(*b*) has been found

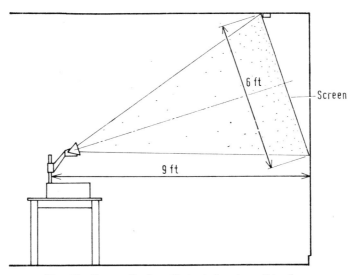

6 ft

9 ft

Screen

FIG. 65. Screen tilted to eliminate keystone distortion

valuable. Using a light-coloured wall instead of a screen adds to the atmosphere of informality so desirable in such work: it is quite adequate for the purpose since a very large image is unnecessary.

Every type of opaque screen gives the best results when no strong direct light reaches it from the front and when it is contained in a black frame. Consequently, if viewing is difficult, the screen should be made the back inside wall of a black box, which is open at the front.

Translucent screens, generally speaking, are more directional than opaque ones, and must be so arranged that no direct light reaches their back surface. They are extraordinarily useful for use with small groups in bright classrooms where, as part of a back-projection arrangement, they can be used without blackout. They are also valuable where space is limited and can often be fitted into the wall or door of a cupboard so that the projector beam can pass to and fro inside the cupboard itself.

122

Fig. 67 shows the area in which a class would view a translucent screen about 3 ft wide. Typical viewing arrangements are shown in *Figs.* 68 to 71.

Models

Conventionally model-making methods are well enough known but for teaching and training it is important not to overlook the value of very simple models in cardboard, balsa wood, soap, string and expanded polystyrene.

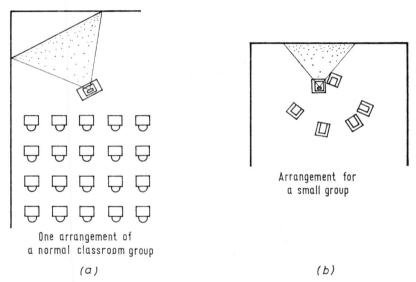

One arrangement of
a normal classroom group

(a)

Arrangement for
a small group

(b)

FIG. 66. (*a*) Angled screen for normal classroom, (*b*) Wall screen for small tutorial meeting

(See Plates 3 and 4.) Polystyrene blocks can be cut as though they were butter with a hot wire or a hot poker and, indeed small electrically heated cutters are marketed for this purpose.

Charts

Paper for chart-making varies in quality from rag paper ("hot pressed" for diagrams and "not pressed" for colour washes) to newsprint; it varies too in thickness, strength and colour. The most generally useful is good quality cartridge paper in imperial (72 lb) sheets which measure 22 in. × 30 in., and coloured Manila card in double crown (100 lb) sheets which measure 20 in. × 30 in. or the corresponding new international paper sizes. If at all possible, paper should not be rolled.

Charts which have been finished in freehand lines very often look more professional than those finished with instruments. For this purpose, felt-tipped pens enable easy strokes to be drawn in quick-drying ink. Water-colour

123

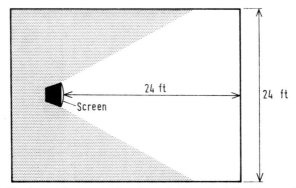

FIG. 67. Approximate area for clear viewing of a 3 ft wide translucent screen in a small classroom

FIG. 68. Normal viewing of an opaque screen

brushes and thick crayons are also useful in this work. Bold straight lines in colour or pattern may be produced very easily with self-adhesive tape. This, and coloured foil, may be cut to size after fixing, by using a razor blade or one of the special cutting knives with a razor-type blade.

Bright colours should be used discreetly and chosen to "bring out" the

Fig. 69(a). Small group viewing a translucent screen

Fig. 69(b). Individual viewing of small screen in library viewing area

significant part of a picture or to draw attention to essential details. Bright red or yellow areas on a pastel grey, blue or white ground are especially effective. Large areas are, generally, best tinted—for which water colours are suitable—with outlines and focal points brightly coloured, say in opaque poster paint. But do remember that most colour-blind people have difficulty in distinguishing certain greens from greys and blues. Where masses of

FIG. 70. Loop film viewing for skill learning

FIG. 71. Corridor showing of loop film on translucent screen

126

colour must be used, as in a column graph for example, cut the required rectangles from Manila board or cloth and stick them to a Manila sheet with, say, Copydex, or for simplicity cut them from self-adhesive sheets of coloured film. A narrow space between the strips accentuates the outline (*Fig.* 72). Lettering often spoils rather than clarifies a chart of this kind, but if lettering is necessary, it may be advisable to stencil, transfer of draw the words on paper strips before attaching them to the drawing. This technique has the dual advantage of preventing damage to the chart through smudging or inaccuracy, and making a preview possible during which the positioning

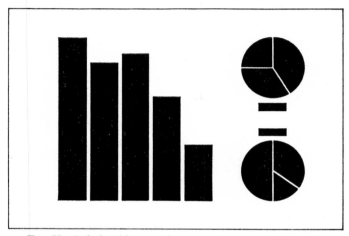

FIG. 72. Relationships are often more important than words

and legibility of the lettering can be correctly estimated under working conditions.

Feltboards

A feltboard is made by stretching a sheet of best quality felt over a chalk-board (or other flat surface) and pinning it at the back. It is good house-keeping to brush it with a stiff brush each time it is used as this not only leaves it with a clean matt surface but roughens it.

Areas of colour, for column graphs or silhouettes, can be cut from felt and need no further preparation. Diagrams, which should be as bold as if they were in chalk on a chalkboard, can be drawn on paper and backed with lint. Good effects are obtained if the diagrams are bounded by a wide, black edge, the surrounding paper cut away, and the finished diagram used with a black backcloth (*Fig.* 73). Lint should be fixed to the back of the paper so that its fluffy side is outwards. To prevent the paper from distorting it is best to use a rubber adhesive such as Copydex.

Enlarged copies of small diagrams can be made with the aid of an episcope. Since the required enlargement is often less than the minimum for which the

127

episcope lens is adjustable, it is usually necessary to remove the lens and support it in front of the instrument. After the diagram has been outlined lightly, the paper can be removed from its vertical position and the work finished in comfort.

Special gridded flock paper which has outstanding adhesive properties is available for feltboard diagrams: in fact some enthusiasts use blotting

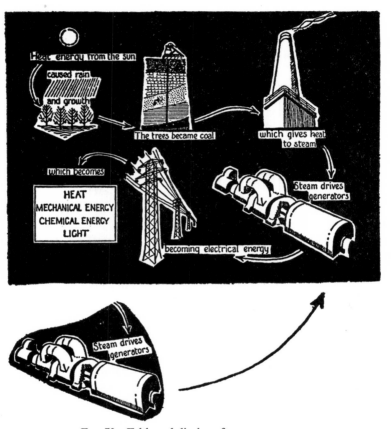

FIG. 73. Feltboard display of energy sequence

paper, glass paper and other materials which will adhere to felt, but it is advisable to begin by using one of two alternatives—felt for silhouettes and lint-backed paper or gridded flock paper for diagrams and headings.

Plastigraph
This is coloured plastic sheeting which can be used in much the same way as felt. Background sheets, which have a smooth working face and matt back, are heavy enough to hang flat under their own weight when supported along

128

their top edges. It is useful to join the top edge to a length of one-inch-diameter dowel so that the sheet can be rolled for storage. In doing this care should be taken to avoid protrusions of any sort or the material will be permanently deformed.

Plastigraph cut-outs are usually made from thinner, very brightly coloured sheet, but for some purposes this may be too highly reflective, when backing sheet can be used, and indeed, looks very attractive. An advantage of the smooth sheets is that any number of layers can be superimposed on one another; a technique of obvious value in illustrating lessons in geology and ecology.

It is advisable not to draw lines directly on the plastic cut-outs but to smooth a transparent Cellophane sheet over the section to be marked and draw on that with wax crayons or felt pens. For fixing paper or card to such diagrams, special stickers are available.

Material which is to be used many times should be stored (flat if possible) in folders or envelopes, and gently wiped with a damp cloth if it ever becomes dusty.

Magnetic Boards

A sheet of medium thickness tinplate, with its corners rounded and its edges rubbed with a file to make them safe, makes a first-class portable magnetic board. This can be painted with a metal primer followed by an undercoat and finishing coat or, for a really permanent surface, given two coats of polyurethane paint. Alternatively it can be covered with Fablon which makes a suitable writing surface for felt pens. If the metal is painted with "blackboard paint" the sheet can be used as both a chalkboard and a magnetic board: painted white it can also serve as a projector screen. Cord for hanging it by should be fixed through two holes drilled in one of its edges. Large permanent boards of black iron sheet can be affixed to a rigid support or, alternatively, the boards are available commercially.

If it is to be used sufficiently often for the same illustration a permanent outline can be painted on the metal or it can be built up from wood laths or hardboard, fixed to the metal with Bostik, and painted. Movable shapes are cut from ply or hardboard and small disc magnets are stuck to them (*Fig.* 74).

"Magnetic" rubber in sheet form can be cut with scissors to make shapes or symbols. Magnetized plastic strip is a useful alternative to disc magnets—not so powerful but cheaper. There is also magnetic "string."

Slides

Two-inch-square slides can be made, either by cutting frames from a filmstrip and mounting them in slide holders, or by taking 35-mm colour photographs and having them processed in the usual way. A convenient technique is to draw diagrams on a chalkboard using coloured chalks and to photograph them on colour transparencies. Amateur photographers are advised to take these pictures out of doors rather than by artificial light as this eliminates exposure difficulties.

Filmstrips
Filmstrips can be made very easily by taking a series of photographs on 35-mm reversal colour film and asking for the film to be returned uncut after being processed. If, however, the originals consist of diagrams and photographs it may be simpler to have the strip made professionally. Material for the

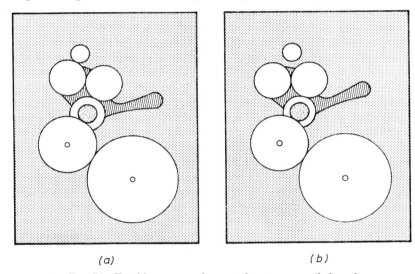

(a)   (b)

Fig. 74. Tumbler gears and gear train on a magnetic board

frames should be collected and mounted, arranged in the required sequence, and numbered. It is then sent to one of the firms which specializes in making filmstrips.

Overhead Projector Illustrations
Transparencies for the overhead projector may be drawn by hand, reproduced by photographic means or built up from cut-out pieces of coloured foil.

Hand-made transparencies are usually prepared on 10-in.-square acetate sheets: these are sold by most aids suppliers. If the slide is in any way complicated, first draw the diagram on paper in the form of a rough layout in order to estimate its best arrangement and most suitable content. If in any doubt about its clarity, trace it on to an acetate sheet with a wax-based pencil (this can be cleaned off afterwards and the sheet used again), project its image on to a screen and see if it is sufficiently clear to be understood from the back of the room in which it will be used. After making any modifications that are called for, complete a fair copy of the diagram on paper and leave

130

any guide-lines which have been drawn. Using drafting tape, fix a transparency over the diagram and trace it.

Much cheaper sheets of a special Cellophane are also available and these can be written on with most of the common writing materials including ball-point pens.

Ink lines can be drawn on acetate with nibs which have flat disc-like ends to them; they are called script nibs. Two kinds of ink are available; etching plastic ink which cannot be erased and non-etching plastic ink which can be.

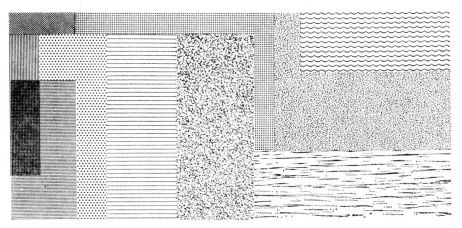

FIG. 75. Shading film

Both are available in a range of transparent colours and also in black. After they have been used, drawing instruments should be cleaned with solvent and a clean rag or soft paper.

Before transparencies are used it is advisable, but not necessary, to mount them in suitable frames; those drawn in pencil or non-etching ink should be protected with cover sheets. Drafting tape, which is self-adhesive, is the best material for fixing film transparencies into card frames.

Drawings can be coloured with plastic ink but it often produces rather disappointing results since the colour generally looks blotchy. Felt-tipped pens may also be used if the shape to be coloured is fairly regular and where clarity is more important than draughtsmanship. Good results may be obtained with sheets of coloured adhesive foils (which vary considerably in quality) and also with some shading film. *Fig.* 75 shows examples of the latter.

To use a coloured or shaded film, cut it to shape and then remove the backing sheet which protects the adhesive surface. Position one edge of the film and, working from that edge, press it into position on the diagram (*Fig.* 76(*a*)). To shade an irregular shape, score around the foil with a sharp knife to produce an area slightly larger than the space to be covered, lift

131

the film from the backing sheet, and press it into position. Finally cut it to the correct shape and remove the surplus film (*Fig.* 76(*b*)). Special razor-sharp pointed knives are made for this work; they are inexpensive and very easy to use.

In addition to self-adhesive sheets, self-adhesive tapes are also available. Transparent tapes in vivid colour are made in widths from $\frac{1}{32}$ in. to 1 in., and there are also tapes marked in a wide range of symbols, lines, numbers and letters.

The special problem of lettering can be simplified by using self-adhesive transfer letters. When these transfers are liable to be handled a great deal,

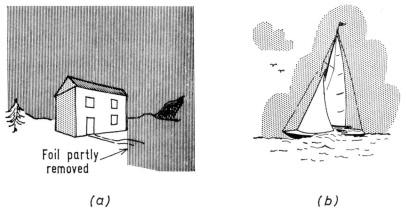

Foil partly removed

(*a*)   (*b*)

FIG. 76. Using shading to heighten interest of illustration

or when they are likely to be exposed to heat, they should be sprayed with Aerosol 101 Protective Coating, or covered with a transparent cover sheet.

One important form of illustration, which is less frequently used than its value deserves, is the silhouette. Pictures cut from journals and newspapers provide useful material for teaching—especially for recognition quizzes—but much more than this can be used. The movement of gears on a machine can be shown in silhouette simply by moving pennies over an outline; the flow on a conveyor, techniques of pruning trees, pattern structure, traffic or ship movement, workshop and office layout may all be illustrated effectively in this way. Cut-outs moved around are extremely useful in language teaching.

COPYING PROCESSES

Detailed and carefully finished illustrations cannot usually be prepared directly on acetate foil by hand. They can, however, be drawn on paper and then transferred to foil by one of a number of copying techniques. *Fig.* 77 is a typical example of such a slide. These methods can also be used to make transparencies from printed originals. They all reproduce black and white

132

material very well indeed; they are generally suitable for coloured line originals and, as a rule, are unsuitable for half-tone photographs.

Four groups of methods are in common use: photocopying on to films of low sensitivity, xerographic printing, the use of films coated with diazonium

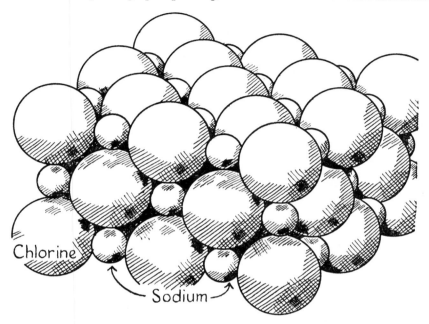

FIG. 77. An overhead projector transparency printed from a carefully drawn original

compounds which are developed by ammonia fumes—the dyeline process—and the use of foils sensitive to heat.

Reflex Photography

Transparencies are produced by this technique in two stages; a paper negative is made first, and this is then used to produce a positive image on film. A copier consists essentially of a light box with a diffusing glass top to it above which is fitted a padded hinged lid. The paper to be exposed is placed on the glass surface, the copy is placed on top of it, face downwards, and the two are pressed flat by clamping the lid on to them. The exposure is set on a dial and it is timed automatically. The exposed negative is "posted" into a slot in the machine from which it is fed by means of rotating rollers through developing and fixing solutions contained inside the machine itself. It emerges very slightly damp and ready for immediate use. Prints are made from the negative in the same way as the negatives are made from the copy except that they are exposed with the negative on the glass surface and the foil above it, i.e. direct as opposed to reflex photography. The developer and fixer are stored separately from the machine which must be cleaned after use.

Transfer Processes
The diffusion transfer process employs a paper negative. The undeveloped negative and the foil are then fed together into a set of rotating rolls which takes them through a developing solution. The feeding mechanism is arranged to hold the sheets apart whilst they are developed and then to squeeze them together as they are delivered (*Fig.* 78). The foil is not light-sensitive;

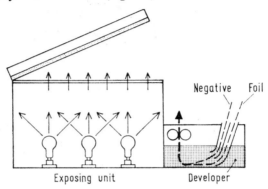

Negative   Foil

Exposing unit   Developer

Fig. 78. Diffusion transfer printer

instead the image is transferred chemically on to the foil at the same time as it is developing in the negative. The two sheets are left in contact with one another for about a minute; they are then stripped apart and the foil washed in water to clear the transparent areas. (Washing is not necessary when the instrument is used to produce copies on opaque paper.)

In this process the negative is usually thrown away immediately the print has been produced and a new negative made if an additional print is needed. A single transparency can be produced in a matter of a minute or so by this method and the process involves only one liquid solution—the developer. It is suitable for all originals except half-tone photographs, although these too can be reproduced if they are first covered with a coarse half-tone screen. Coloured lines copy as black ones and there is some loss in the density with which yellow and green lines reproduce. The developer must be stored separately from the machine, which should be washed out after use.

Xerography is mentioned because many organizations use the equipment for office printing. The photo-surface in xerography is an electrostatically charged plate. Where light falls on it, the surface is discharged. Consequently, when the plate is exposed in a camera, a negative consisting of lines of static charge is formed. This plate is powdered, and the powder sticks to the lines of charge just as it would to the surface of a rubbed fountain pen. A charged

134

sheet of transparent foil is now placed over the negative; this pulls the powder off the plate and a positive image is formed. The image is fixed in a vapour box. This equipment will produce enlarged or reduced prints. Not all Xerox machines are suitable for transparencies and consequently it is wise to consult Rank Xerox if in doubt.

Dyeline Copying
The dyeline method of photocopying makes use of foils coated with diazonium compounds which, when exposed in ammonia vapour, develop images in

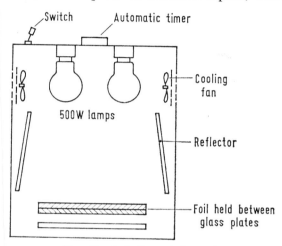

FIG. 79. A dyeline printing unit

one of a wide range of colours. The compound is bleached out when it is exposed to ultra-violet light.

The printer consists of a light-box with a negative holder in its base (*Fig.* 79). The simplest kind of developing unit is a large sweet jar containing an ounce or two of 0·880 ammonia: the liquid is usually covered with metal gauze to prevent it from wetting the foils. More sophisticated units are, of course, available.

Originals must be prepared on translucent or transparent material, for example on tracing paper. This is placed, face down, on the sensitive surface of a foil and pressed flat beneath a glass plate. It is exposed for about two minutes and then developed in the ammonia vapour for about the same time.

With this equipment composite diagrams in a number of colours can be produced. For example, two transparencies can be made, one with a blue diagram on it and the second with a red one, so that when they are superimposed one on the other, the two sections are differentiated by the colours.

The obvious way of producing such a set of transparencies is illustrated in *Fig.* 80. Here, the original is drawn in pencil and two separate tracings

135

(*a*) and (*b*) made from it. These can be in black pencil or in Indian ink. A print is taken from (*a*) on a "blue" foil and this produces a blue diagram on a transparent background. A "red" print is made from (*b*).

Fig. 81 illustrates a more mechanical method which eliminates the labour of tracing. Here, the original (*Fig.* 81(*a*)) is drawn on translucent paper and

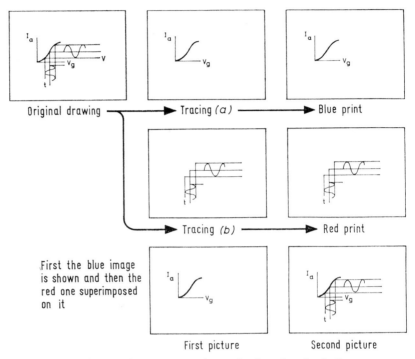

FIG. 80. Producing a two-colour pair of overlays by dyeline

three prints made from it on to "pale blue" dyeline paper (*Fig.* 81(*b*)). This gives three translucent copies of the original in pale blue lines, and dyeline foils are insensitive to pale blue. Consequently, parts which are to be reproduced are picked out in black as shown (*Fig.* 81(*c*)). These are then printed on foils of different colours (*Fig.* 81(*d*)) so that when they are superimposed a multi-coloured diagram results (*Fig.* 81(*e*)).

Thermal Copying

In this process, foils which are insensitive to light but sensitive to heat are used. In principle, the copy is covered by the foil and the two are pressed together and heated. Heat is absorbed by the dark lines of the copy but it is reflected from the lighter areas and consequently the foil is "printed" with the image of the original. The process is clean, quick and simple: each print is made in about four seconds. Originals in red, green and orange do not reproduce well, but apart from this almost any line originals—transparent, translucent or opaque—can be used. Several originals can be combined on one transparency by feeding them through the machine in turn.

Thermal copying is probably the most flexible of the copying processes—transparencies can even be produced during a lesson. No other method could be more simple. Foils of many kinds are available from those giving black images on a transparent ground, to coloured foils giving transparent images

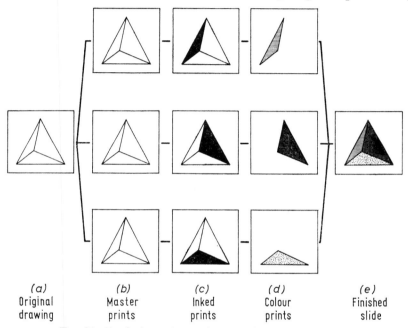

(a)	(b)	(c)	(d)	(e)
Original	Master	Inked	Colour	Finished
drawing	prints	prints	prints	slide

FIG. 81. Producing a three-colour set of overlays by dyeline

and transparent foils giving coloured images. Roller copiers are available for making prints from sheets and flat-bed copiers for making prints from either sheets or books.

In addition to these common methods of producing transparencies there are others which include transferring to transparent film in a duplicating machine and using an electronic stencil-cutting machine.

METHODS OF USING TRANSPARENCIES

Transparencies can, of course, take the place of teaching charts. To this end their presentation should be as unobtrusive as possible. One way to ensure this is to place the slide in position beforehand and not to switch the projector on until the picture is needed. When it has served its purpose the projector

Outline
black

Towns
red

Rivers
blue

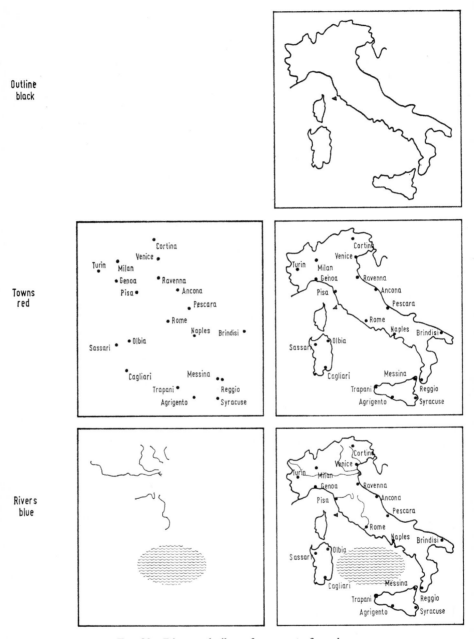

FIG. 82. Diagram built up from a set of overlays

138

should be switched off again and the transparency removed. It is often helpful to supplement the diagram as it is being explained. This can be done without damaging the transparency itself by using a cover sheet of clear acetate on which to make the additional markings or by sliding the transparency beneath an acetate roll and writing on that.

When diagrams are built up by using a set of overlays (*Fig.* 82) it is usually best to keep the projector switched on until the final diagram in the sequence is in place. This integrates the visual presentation with the verbal: indeed

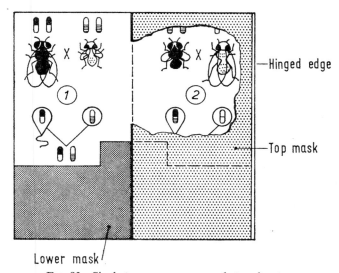

Fig. 83. Single transparency exposed stage by stage

in most instances, since the visuals form the focus of the learner's attention, the verbal description should be concise and supplementary—in a manner of a commentary. Extended information which is given during a sequence of this nature is more likely to confuse than it is to help. Similar considerations apply when a single diagram is being uncovered stage by stage (*Fig.* 83).

On the contrary, when a set of overlays is used to present separate items which subsequently will be used to make a visual summary of a lesson, the instrument should be switched on only whilst each addition is made: in this way the full power of the visual is used in the recapitulation (*Fig.* 84).

Books of transparencies are now available commercially. These fit into a frame and any selected sets of overlays can be shown to illustrate a lesson (*Fig.* 85).

Moving Diagrams
These are a logical extension of the overlay technique. Chess moves, for instance, would be shown with opaque shapes for the black pieces and, say,

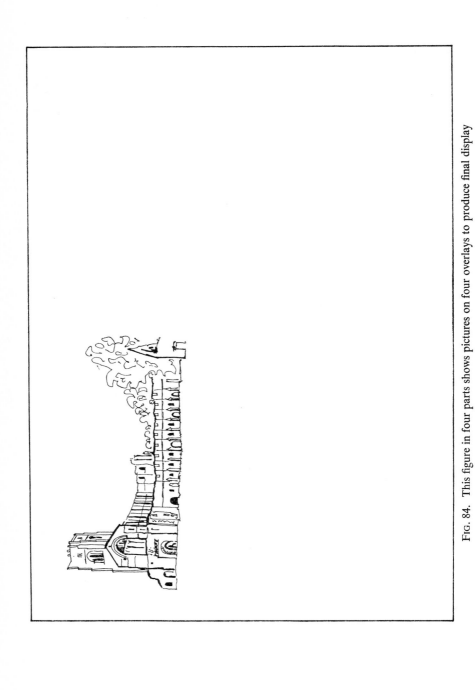

Fig. 84. This figure in four parts shows pictures on four overlays to produce final display

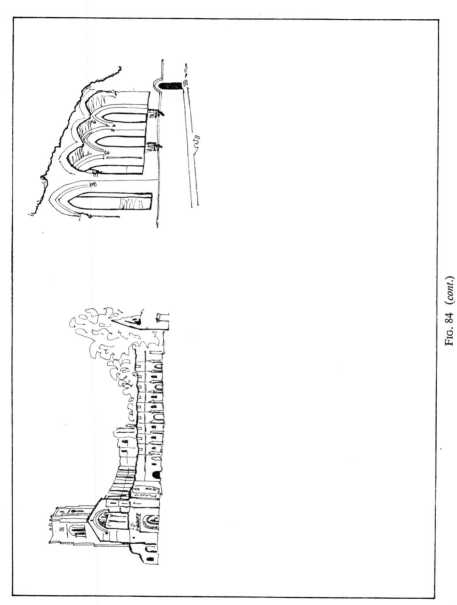

Fig. 84 (cont.)

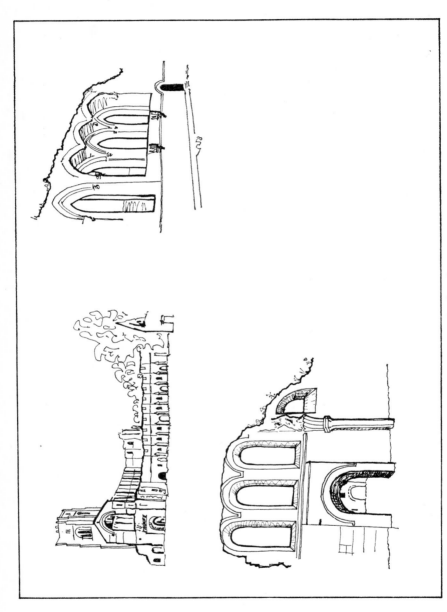

FIG. 84 (cont.)

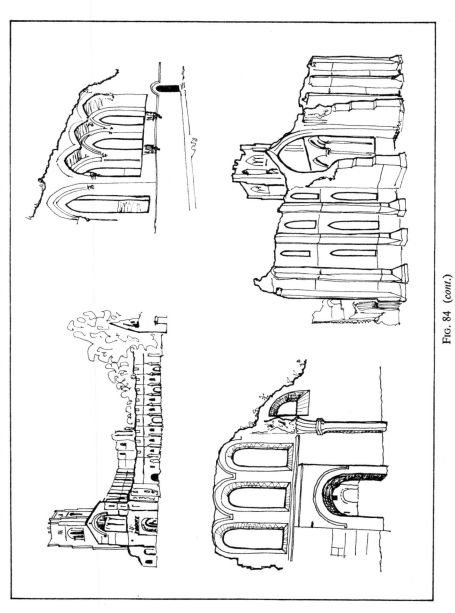

FIG. 84 (cont.)

transparent yellow shapes for the white ones, moved on a chessboard grid. Navigational problems, flow diagrams, work-study examples, layout exercises are a few of the fields in which this technique has an obvious application. *Fig.* 86 shows a piece of elastic used to show the line of a stream of electrons.

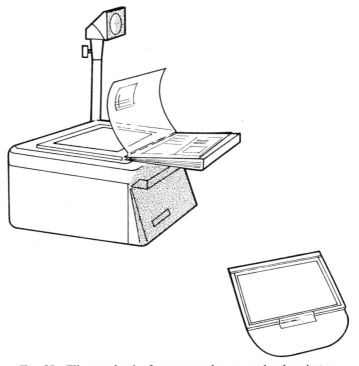

FIG. 85. Flipatran book of transparencies on overhead projectors

When one or two parts of a mechanism swivel or rotate, the diagram may be drawn on one foil and the moving part on another: a paper clip may then be used as the pivot. *Fig.* 87 shows one type of diagram which, because it illustrates changes as the teacher describes them, can make a powerful contribution to the development of insight into relationships which students might otherwise find elusive. *Fig.* 88 is a moving diagram which shows on the screen as a silhouette.

WORKING MODELS

Diagrams which are built from card, Perspex and so on are really two-dimensional working models: they are seen on the screen as moving diagrams. Models of mechanisms may be made on a Perspex back-plate and outlined in, say, balsa wood and fixed in position with balsa cement. The wood, which can be bought already cut in strips of convenient widths, should be coated with a transparent hardener such as Bourne Seal after it has been

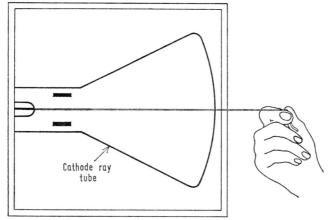

FIG. 86. A "movable" beam of cathode rays

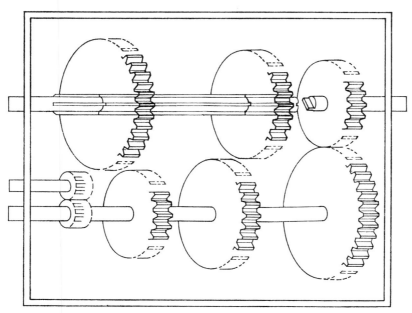

FIG. 87. A three-speed gear diagram in which the gears slide in and out of mesh when the acetate overlays are moved in their slides

fitted. *Fig.* 89 shows one such model which is used in teaching the four-stroke cycle of a petrol engine. More sophisticated devices can be made in metal or Perspex (*Fig.* 90), but the advantage of authenticity should be

145

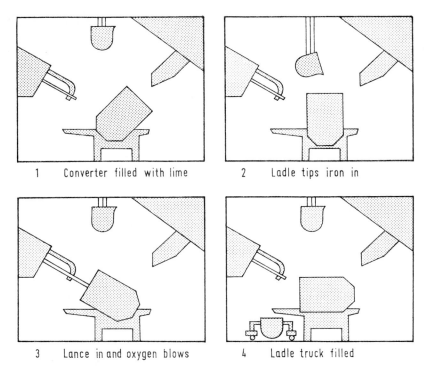

1   Converter filled with lime

2   Ladle tips iron in

3   Lance in and oxygen blows

4   Ladle truck filled

FIG. 88. Movement of a silhouette produced by sliding and rotating card shapes

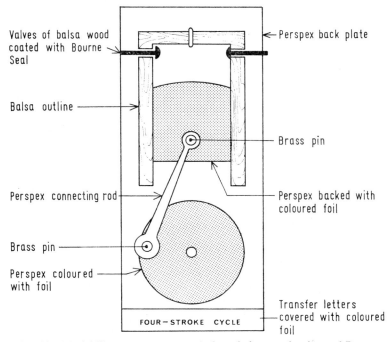

Valves of balsa wood coated with Bourne Seal

Perspex back plate

Balsa outline

Brass pin

Perspex connecting rod

Perspex backed with coloured foil

Brass pin

Perspex coloured with foil

FOUR—STROKE CYCLE

Transfer letters covered with coloured foil

FIG. 89. Model-like transparency made from balsa wood strips and Perspex

weighed against the extremely important factor of teacher involvement. Where the teacher is seen to move and adjust the diagram as he explains it, students will usually make more effort to create the insight which the presentation is designed to evoke. Often a perfect mechanical presentation seems to students to have done the hard work for them and they relax into a feeling of quite false intellectual security. This is a danger in all forms of highly polished presentation. Meccano parts fixed to a perforated Perspex plate are among the many ready-made materials which can be used for working

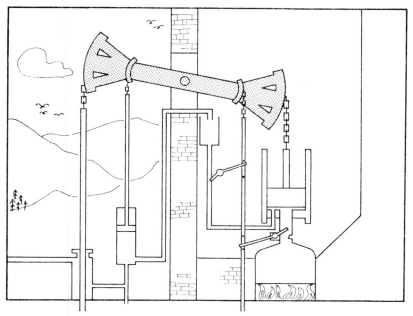

FIG. 90. Model in Perspex and brass of a Newcomen Atmospheric Engine. The valve movements are controlled by elastic bands (not shown)

model equipment. *Fig.* 91 shows them made up as a pulley system which, on the screen, moves with a velocity ratio of four.

DEMONSTRATIONS

Some demonstrations can be projected as they are performed. Magnetic fields using either a pocket compass which has a glass base or iron filings, electric fields using grass seed floating on oil in a shallow glass dish, colour changes of indicators, polarized light using two sheets of Polaroid, effects of colour and the formation of precipitates or crystals are obvious examples. This application eliminates straining to see or the alternative of repeated demonstrations to small groups.

147

The smaller projectors can usually work as well lying on one side as they can standing on their bases. This opens up the possibility of projecting demonstrations which can be performed only in a vertical plane such as, for example, the damping effect of a magnetic field on a swinging conductor. In this case the image is inverted but this is of no consequence.

In such demonstrations as, for example, the experiment to show the formation of drops, or some of the surface tension effects, the image should not be "upside down." This can be remedied by using a plane mirror to reverse

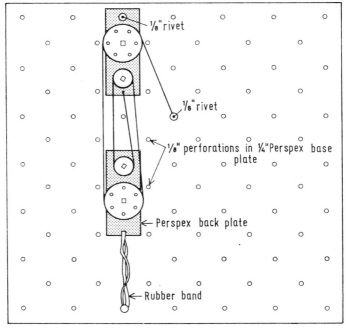

FIG. 91. Meccano components on a perforated Perspex plate

the beam direction and consequently to reinvert the image (*Fig.* 92). If the image is thrown on the ceiling, the upside-down effect is not apparent.

Fig. 93 shows a ripple tank which is particularly valuable for the demonstration of wave phenomena. Each edge of the tank may be covered with a lint strip to prevent reflections, and water poured in it to a depth of about three-eighths of an inch. Circular ripples can be produced by allowing water drops to fall into the tank from a dropper, whilst trains of parallel waves may be made by rolling a one-inch diameter wooden rod very slightly to and fro in the water. Refraction effects can be demonstrated by putting a Perspex or glass triangle (about one-quarter of an inch thick) in the tank to simulate a transparent block. Rubber tubing makes excellent reflecting surfaces whilst diffraction and interference effects may be effectively and simply demonstrated.

148

One very important development is the introduction of multi-range transparent electric meters by the AVO Company. These for the first time enable demonstrations of electrical phenomena to be presented quantitatively

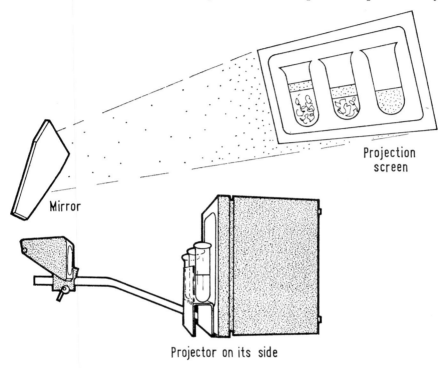

Projection
screen

Mirror

Projector on its side

Fig. 92. Projector set for demonstration of experiment which cannot be performed on a horizontal plane

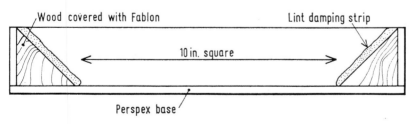

Wood covered with Fablon

Lint damping strip

10 in. square

Perspex base

Fig. 93. Section of a ripple tank

to groups of almost any size. In most laboratories and science lecture rooms this facility alone would justify the purchase of an overhead projector. The following three courses may be followed: first the circuit may be designed for, and set up on, the overhead projector itself, a technique which is limited by the size of the instrument; secondly the projector may be used to show only the meters, whilst the rest of the apparatus is built large enough for the group to see; thirdly the meters can be on the projector and the rest of the equipment alongside but, as the equipment is explained, it can be drawn as

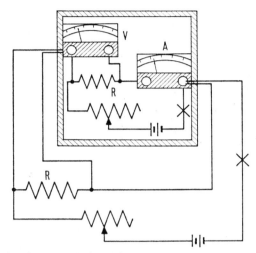

FIG. 94. Electric meters designed for use on an overhead projector (AVO)

a circuit on the projector itself in such a way as to incorporate the actual meters (*Fig.* 94).

MAKING LOOP FILMS

To supplement professionally made loop films, teachers can make their own by shooting the film and having it loaded into cassettes for a matter of a few shillings. For this purpose, they need a camera, a splicer for joining film, an editor for viewing the film preparatory to splicing it, a stable tripod and lights. Methods of making and editing film are fully described in many photographic handbooks and the techniques are well within the scope of anyone who is interested.

The professional problem for the teacher is that of preparing a good script from which the film will be shot. It is important to realize the essential difference between the loop film and the normal film: the former runs over and over again until the projector is switched off whilst the latter has a beginning and end to it. One obvious subject is therefore an object which needs viewing from all sides: this can be filmed as it rotates on a slowly rotating turntable.

Apart from this simple viewing film, all others should be composed on paper prior to filming. It is wise to begin by writing down for whom the film is intended and what it is to teach. Next the film content is broken down into single elements and each one tested to ensure that it does not consist of simpler ones. From this a story-board can be prepared on which each step is arranged, rearranged, removed or supplemented until the film satisfies the producer.

Since loops are viewed over and over again, they can help learners to establish associations and appreciate relationships and this can be prepared for. Take, for example, a loop which aims to teach students how to identify zones in the upper chalk from the zone fossils. Such a loop should provide links from the particular to the general: from the geology of Britain, to S.E. England, to the chalk face, to the upper chalk, to the zone fossil. And when the film starts again it will link the zone fossil with Great Britain which, therefore should be drawn with the upper chalk areas clearly marked. The story-board for this loop would appear as shown in *Fig. 95*.

Simple association, such as relating a name with a flower and its habitat can be assisted by a series of lap-dissolves, that is with one picture fading into a new one (*Fig. 96*).

It may be desirable to include titles or diagrams in loop films but it should be remembered that the reason for using film is to show movement or change. If many diagrams are used it may be that the topic is more suitable for slides.

Sound can be added to 8-mm film if its edge is first stripped with a band of magnetic material. However, one of the great values of a loop film is that it enables the teacher to use a series of commentaries and techniques as it repeats and, unless it is to be used for private study a sound track may be an unnecessary expense.

USING LOOP FILM

There is quite obviously a connexion between the use which can be made of a loop film and its form and content. And although we should not make hard-and-fast rules about this because learning abilities and peculiarities are so varied, the film maker or purchaser should keep certain purposes in mind when assessing the suitability of the content of a film.

In the first place it is useful to decide whether the loop will be used mainly to supplement classroom teaching or mainly for private study. For the former it is a teaching aid and can be incomplete in itself: it will show what is best learned from film and the teacher will provide it with a relevant context. For the latter it must be complete in itself or made complete by the use of supplementary material. Its context must be clear and any support which is necessary to the visuals must be provided by captions on the film, by notes which preferably should be in the form of a programme, by a taped commentary or by books and so on. These references should be given on the loop itself so that the viewer knows the visual is incomplete without them.

151

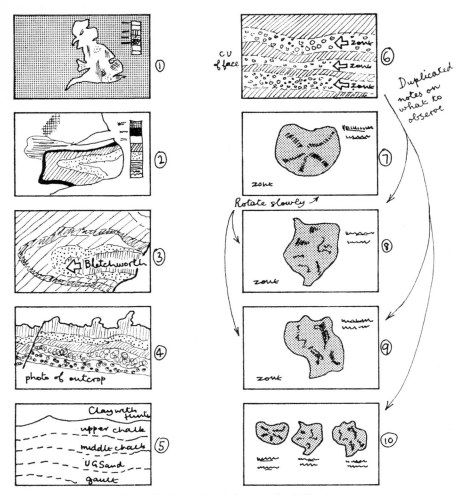

FIG. 95. Story-board for zone-fossil film loop

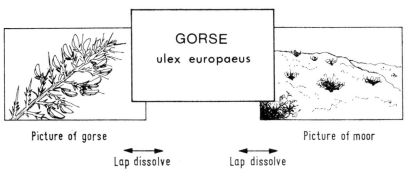

FIG. 96. Association by visual overlap

Thus, whilst loops for classroom teaching may also be available in the audio-visual section of a library, care must be taken to provide for the different roles of teaching *aid* on the one hand and teaching *device* on the other.

There are four main areas in which loop films can enhance learning. The first is in presenting facts: in showing what things look like, what happens, how something is done, and so on. The second is to teach or aid the teaching of a skill. The third is to assist the formation of a concept and the fourth is to present a problem for solution. There is, of course, an inevitable overlap here, but loops are of such short duration that their main function should be quite evident and they should be used in such a way as to emphasize this function.

INDEXING AND PRESERVING MATERIAL

In order to derive a full return from the amount of time and material invested in teaching aids, some attention should be given to storing them wisely. Because of their cost, films may be hired when they are needed, or bought and stored centrally. It is essential that every potential user should have precise and up-to-date instructions on how to obtain and show a film: he should have access to up-to-date catalogues. The considerable number of teachers who do not know how to hire and use films, even though they are employed by authorities with progressive aids policies, demonstrates beyond any doubt that provision of opportunity is not enough. Because films are returned immediately after they have been used, brief comments on them kept in a card-index file can be valuable.

Filmstrips can be stored centrally in one of the special cabinets designed for this purpose; there must also be a corresponding file for the notes. Somebody, preferably a librarian, should be responsible for the collection or it will become muddled and dispersed. The strips should be classified in the same way as library books—if there is no library a simplified version of the Dewey system can be prepared and will serve admirably. However, experience suggests that people like to be responsible for, at any rate, some strips which they find very useful and consequently, if cost is no handicap, it is better to meet this preference. Again, a card index is essential if filmstrips are stored centrally and useful if they are kept individually.

Without an efficient custodian, and a good system of classification, centrally stored slides are a waste of money and space. Every year the collection should be ruthlessly culled and the records altered accordingly; left to grow naturally, a teaching-slide collection becomes unwieldy and so depressing that folk avoid it. One excellent method is to store the slides in slide magazines. When one or more slides are required, the whole magazine is issued, the slides shown and the magazine returned without being opened.

Charts are best stored open and hanging, a useful method being to punch and reinforce two holes in their top edges and slide them over pegs fixed to a wall. Again, once a chart is no longer of use it should be destroyed. Valuable pictures can be stored in plastic envelopes or mounted on board and varnished. They can be covered with a transparent self-adhesive plastic film which is available either with a matt or a glossy surface and which is simply smoothed on to the chart to which it sticks.

Episcope pictures can be mounted on standardized black cards and indexed in the usual way. Where diagrams in a book have been found useful, white cards referring to them can be inserted in the index.

Felt diagrams, plastigraph diagrams and cut-outs for magnetic boards can be kept in a foolscap or quarto filing cabinet, each group in a Manila folder.

Overhead projector transparencies in book form are perfectly suited to storage in a library as are boxed loop films.

REFERENCES

1. LUNZER, E. A., *Recent Studies in Britain Based on the Work of Jean Piaget*, N.F.E.R., p. 15.

FURTHER READING

H.M.S.O., *Audio-Visual Aids in Higher Scientific Education*, 1963, 153 pp.

ATKINSON, NORMAN J., *Modern Teaching Aids*, London, Maclaren, 1966, 208 pp.

BROWN, JAMES W. and THORNTON JR., JAMES W., *New Media in Higher Education*, Association for Higher Education of the National Education Association, Washington, 1963, 182 pp.

INDUSTRIAL SOCIETY, THE, *Using Sound Filmstrips*, 1962, 40 pp.

KODAK, *The Fundamentals of Film Making* (booklet).

NATIONAL COMMITTEE FOR AUDIO-VISUAL AIDS IN EDUCATION, *Visual Education* (monthly). In particular the yearbook (July).

POWELL, G. H. and POWELL, L. S., *A Guide to the 8-mm Loop Film*, BACIE, 1967.

POWELL, L. S., *A Guide to the Overhead Projector*, BACIE, 1964.

POWELL, L. S., *A Guide to the Use of Visual Aids*, BACIE, 1961.

SIMPSON, MARGARET, *Film Projecting: without Tears or Technicalities*, National Committee for Audio-Visual Aids in Education, 1966, 51 pp.

TAYLOR, E. A., *A Manual of Visual Presentation in Education and Training*, London, Pergamon, 1966.

8 EDUCATIONAL TELEVISION

Educational television has been extensively researched over and we now know a good deal about its characteristics as a communication device. In some fields outside the formal educational ones it is undoubtedly both powerful and persuasive whilst in others it amounts to no more than "the chewing gum of the eyes," to quote Frank Lloyd Wright. In education we find wide divergencies too. Telescuola's, "It's Never too Late" in Italy has taught thousands of illiterates to read and write. With the aid of television, Japan has achieved nationwide literacy and has moved on to utilize the medium to an impressive degree. In his survey published by the British Film Institute in 1967,[1] John Scupham reports, for example, that the Japanese training programme for young farmers called "Agriculture Classroom" reaches 300,000 people. He adds, "As with the programmes for schools it is the sheer weight of the Japanese effort that is most impressive." And Japan is doing very well. In America, with well over two million school viewers, the Ford Foundation's Report for 1967 quotes one expert as saying that, "if something happened tomorrow to wipe out all instructional television, American schools and colleges would hardly know it was gone."

The forces which press the claims of television are strong and various, from vested interests to teachers whose hearts, for one reason or another, are in electronic circuitry. Whatever these claims may be they must ultimately be weighed against the question, "What would viewers have learned otherwise?" and if the alternative can be shown to be of greater educational consequence there is no valid reason for extolling the virtues of television as "best."

At its worst, educational television can enable an inept teacher to broadcast ill-conceived lessons to far more students than could otherwise receive them: at its best it can disseminate material which has been gathered from many sources and organized with the combined foresight and knowledge of a balanced team of wise teachers to classes of students who have already been prepared for learning and motivated to respond actively to the learning once it has been acquired.

155

BROADCAST LESSONS

Broadcast educational television programmes in this country are of a very high standard. In general they are designed to provide learners with a broad background of audio-visual experience relevant to certain areas of knowledge rather than to teach lessons as part of a syllabus. Such programmes are called enrichment broadcasts and their nature makes them appropriate for a range of different courses and for learning by different methods. Such broadcasts must be seen as a context into which lessons fit; as giving more meaning and relevance to study. They will, in general, be seen very near the start of lessons as general introductions to the more closely focused material to be taught by the teacher. Students should not be expected to "learn" them but to be better able to learn because of them, and consequently the test of their value is to be sought in the enhanced liveliness and motivation of the students. If they make the lessons more memorable experiences and even if they make no difference to the amount of syllabus content learned, they will have made a proper contribution to the educative value of the lessons.

A possible structure of a television-assisted lesson would be:

1. Statement by teacher of purpose of lesson directing attention to the parts of the broadcast likely to be of major consequence.
2. Broadcast.
3. Selection by the teacher of that aspect of the broadcast which the lesson is intended to develop and emphasizing it.
4. Lesson by teacher against the "whole" background of the broadcast.
5. Testing of 4, conclusion and reference forward to next lesson.

Some programmes, however, are designed to teach subject matter as part of a coherent syllabus: language lessons, certain mathematics lessons and certain science lessons, for example, and are called direct teaching broadcasts. Research suggests that pupils favour direct teaching lessons to enrichment lessons.[1] Direct teaching broadcasts should integrate closely with the presentation stage of the lesson and the teacher must plan his teaching to absorb the broadcast. He must read the prepared notes before he plans his work and design his progressive and terminal tests to fit the pace of the series. Any variations he may introduce will be in depth rather than in content. A lesson built to accommodate a direct teaching broadcast might have the following structure:

1. General introduction linking with previous lesson.
2. Lead-in to broadcast.
3. Direct teaching by television.
4. Activity designed to follow (amplify, consolidate or practice) the learning which has taken place.
5. Testing of 4.
6. Recapitulation of lesson and preparation for next lesson.

If the broadcast fails to teach the subject matter as effectively as a teacher it has failed. Research shows that follow-up work after a television lesson is vital to its success.[2]

The outstanding quality of television, whether broadcast or closed circuit is that it can provide very large groups with the kind of teaching which is appropriate with small groups: there can be face-to-face teaching, things can happen close to hand, the teacher and the learner can see the same things together, even the image in a microscope. And from a psychological view-point, the small group bondings are more likely to include the teacher if he watches as a learner than when he performs as a teacher—this was especially evident in the early work of Professor Harvey White.[3]

Research also shows that the optimum viewing time during a television lesson is about twenty-five minutes and that the sound must be closely integrated with the visual presentation for maximum effectiveness.

Unfortunately, the assessments made by teachers themselves of the value of broadcast television programmes are outstandingly inconsistent and appear to reflect their personality and competency differences rather than differences in the values of the programmes themselves. Consequently research findings are of critical value in making judgements in this field.

Barrington (1965) has carried out an extensive survey of researches, both in this country and abroad, in the field of instructional television. The following are two of the main conclusions he draws from his survey:

1. There appears to be no significant difference in achievement between pupils taught by television and by conventional methods.
2. The few experiments aimed at measuring the intangibles of the learning situation have also failed to discover significant differences between television taught and conventionally taught pupils.

Macfarlane Smith (1965) has carried out three experiments on the impact of the television broadcasts on the G courses in Engineering Science.[4] The appropriate testing was carried out at the ends of the college sessions in 1963, 1964 and 1965. He writes:

"The trend of the results, taken as a whole, suggests that the television broadcasts had a positive effect both on the attainments of the students and on their attitudes. Differences in scores on attainment and attitude tests usually favoured the groups of students who had seen the television broad-casts, though only in some cases were the differences statistically significant. In the third experiment which involved testing 862 students in 27 colleges, differences in attainment and attitude were most marked in the case of students taking G* courses and these differences favoured the groups which had seen the television broadcasts. The two groups were well-matched in respect of general ability. The difference in attainment was greatest in

157

the section of the test on mechanics, though not quite significant. In the sections on heat and electricity the differences were small and non-significant.

"In the third experiment, while the overall differences for all students from 27 colleges were non-significant, an analysis of the scores for a sample of students from the *eight* colleges which had both television taught and non-television taught classes yielded significant differences in both attitude and attainment. These differences were *all* in favour of the television taught students and were significant at the level $P < 0.05$.

"In this sample the television broadcasts appeared to have a greater impact on students who are above average in ability. There was a striking contrast between the level of significance of the differences between mean scores for attainment and attitude of the experimental and control groups of students at different ability levels. While the experimental groups tended to have higher mean scores for attainment and attitude at all levels, the differences were significant for students in the upper half of the ability range while none of the differences were significant for students in the lower half."

The inference which can be drawn from this is that the time occupied by the broadcasts was either as usefully or more usefully employed by the television than by the teachers of the control groups. Sufficient similar conclusions have been drawn to lead to a general view that good television, properly integrated with classroom teaching, improves the quality of the learning experience by giving the subject matter a greater vitality and flexibility. Other advantages which have been claimed for it include

1. It reduces the total perceptual load by selective focusing.
2. It gives valuable training in observation.
3. It provides teachers with in-service training and fresh ideas.

CLOSED CIRCUIT TELEVISION

The fact that broadcast educational television must be designed for a very large heterogeneous audience is one of its great strengths—it can be generously conceived—and one of its great weaknesses—it cannot be closely concerned with the needs of one particular learning community. This weakness can be eliminated by the community itself operating its own self-contained television system: a closed circuit television system. Although most such systems are, indeed, pieces of apparatus joined into the same circuit by wires, some include short micro-wave links in which the signals are transmitted and received by aerials.

Closed circuit television may be used to link the learning centres of whole cities, a group of buildings or a single building.

City-wide closed circuit television has the same characteristics as broadcast television except that it has much less professional weight behind it however outstanding a few of its specialists may be, and a much closer knowledge of the needs and abilities of its viewers. The authority responsible for it can exert pressures on teachers to organize their work to suit the television lessons, and teachers will tend to associate competency in this more public aspect of teaching with socially recognized success. It is likely to be regarded as valuable because its high costs must be explained and accounted for. The fact that its administrators are the only well paid public educationists whose contribution to classroom learning is constantly assessed by an audience competent to judge should result in some interesting operant conditioning of a useful kind.

The advantages of the system are:

1. It gives teachers reference standards against which to measure the quality of their own work: it can keep them up to date.
2. It can help offset the shortage of specialist teachers.
3. It can guide the development of novel methods and provide teachers with reliable support when they include new subject material in their syllabuses.
4. It can form the basis of inter-staff discussions.
5. It can bring together a greater variety and complexity of equipment, aids and information than a teacher on his own.
6. It has the quality of immediacy.
7. It has authority.
8. It can focus attention closely and for a relatively long time.
9. It does not introduce extraneous mechanical noise into the room or involve any special viewing arrangements.
10. Since it is under the same controlling authority as the teachers, previews and timetables can be catered for, training rationalized, abilities and effort rewarded and minorities considered professionally instead of economically.

Since the programmes are received from "outside" the schools, they will be assessed for technical quality against those broadcast over the national networks. Consequently the studios and equipment should be sophisticated enough to meet this expectation. The programmes, on the other hand, should be seen as "our" programmes and the presenters accepted as "our" staff. Experience indicates that this need is best met by training a pool of teachers in the art and skills of television presentation and selecting the broadcasting teams from this pool.

It is perhaps unfortunate that much of the training in this field is geared to the production of programmes which are measured, not only in quality but also in form, against broadcast programmes. The result of this is that programmes are designed, rehearsed and perfected technically and then the lessons

159

fitted around them. The criteria by which they are judged then become technical ones—the lighting, the shot angles, the sound quality—and the educative value of the experience takes a second place.

The considerable body of knowledge we already possess about the form and content of excellent teaching could constitute the base from which training for closed circuit television begins. Thus, within an existing and tested lesson there may be a need for audio-visual supplementation which can best be met by television and television is therefore fitted in: the television content would then grow organically, as it were, and provide what it is best fitted to provide. Programmes of this kind might then consist of, say, two minutes' presentation, ten minutes' black screen, five minutes' presentation, fifteen minutes' black screen, and so on; an impossible arrangement for the public companies.

The ILEA, in order to foster the maximum co-operation in television teaching, continuously runs preliminary two-day courses open to all teachers and, indeed, to technician assistants. These give a general idea of the kind of equipment involved in the work, a little experience of handling it and a brief experience of devising and presenting a television lesson. Those who stop at this stage have a sufficient idea of the process to receive programmes with a heightened and better informed understanding. Those who wish to continue, take a week's course where they learn the basic skills of scripting, presenting and directing programmes. Those who appear to have a special aptitude for the work are then invited to attend for a further period of about three months to be groomed for seconding to the studios for a period of up to two years.

Campus television has a different function: it serves a number of colleges or schools or training departments on the same site. The special advantage it offers is largely an economic one: staff, equipment and facilities can be shared with a minimum of organizational inconvenience. In an industrial setting it can provide a link between training sections and production areas, enhancing the relevance of the former by correlation with the latter. Inevitably it must be used by teams of staff working very closely together: administration staff, teaching staff, technical, clerical and graphics staff. This team activity, valuable in itself, can lead to a more efficient employment of more talented staff. Generally speaking campus television equipment will include two mobile cameras, a studio with three cameras, a video tape recorder, telecine and full supporting equipment. The staff associated with it may be a director of educational services, responsible for equipment and organization, a programme advisor, two camera-operating technicians and a graphics artist. One figure sometimes heard is that there should be one technician for every £7,000 worth of equipment.

A team of this strength would be inefficiently exploited if it were concerned only with programme production for colleagues. It would therefore also be responsible for all the major teaching equipment in the college as a whole, for training, information and advice on utilization of equipment and with the educational and economic viability of the teaching in which they become involved: it could become a "teaching commando" group.

House television at its most modest is a straightforward teaching aid—possibly no more than a camera and a TV receiver used as a monitor (*Fig.* 97(*a*)).

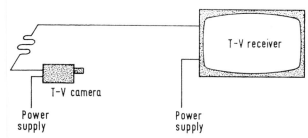

FIG. 97(*a*). The simplest television camera chain

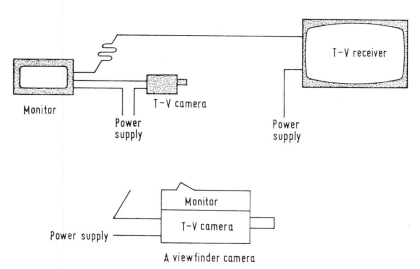

FIG. 97(*b*). Camera with separate (or integrated) operator's monitor

It may be used as an episcope to show diagrams more clearly than an episcope can show them, as a micro-viewer for displaying things which are too small to be seen, like a micro-projector for slides seen through a microscope, to look in safety at dangerous processes and to show things which cannot be moved into lecture rooms or which cannot conveniently be reached by the learners.

161

With practice, a simple set of equipment of this kind can be used almost as naturally and unobtrusively as a chalkboard: as self-consciousness fades the full value of the device emerges. Then, it can be used to offset some long-standing problems. For example, in certain courses, learners are required to set up and use large and costly equipment for laboratory practical work. Because of their cost and size, only single items of these are available and, traditionally, students use them on a rota system. Consequently they are frequently engaged in practical work, the purposes of which they do not fully understand and consequently much of the educative value of the activity is lost.

With a camera focused on the instrument dials or measuring instruments, all students in a group can take readings from the monitor screens as they are indicated. In turn they can manipulate the equipment sufficiently to know about it and understand how to use it and for the rest of the time they prepare their results and reports and participate in discussion with the lecturer. This multiplies, as it were, the availability of expensive equipment and makes possible the proper correlation of theory and practice. In the same way, experiments in rather inaccessible places—the nose of an aircraft or the propeller tunnel of a ship—can be valuable group experiments instead of lonely and time-consuming ones. This might call for the addition of a monitor to enable the camera to be adjusted with precision (*Fig.* 97(*b*)).

The addition of a video tape recorder—an instrument which records television in the same way as a tape recorder records sound—offers two major facilities, the opportunity to play back televised material and what amounts to an audio-visual mirror in which people can see themselves as they are seen by others. This latter facility is of considerable value in those learning activities which involve role-playing exercises such as teacher-training, interviewing, sales training and modelling and can play a part in skill training of various kinds (Plate 5). The value of the playback of role-playing work is greatest when it is done immediately and accompanied by professional guidance and discussion, as this can give the trainee an immediate reinforcement of his good techniques and correction of his bad ones in a success-directed social setting.

This method does not involve the employment of ancillary staff and is naturally and immediately accepted as a useful and down-to-earth learning tool. Experience suggests that the camera for this work is best fitted with a zoom lens and, although the picture quality cannot be ignored, it seems to have only the same significance as the reflective power of a mirror: if you really *do* want to know whether your slip is showing, a shop window will suit admirably.

Single camera sets used in large lecture halls or for overflow meetings are generally expensive pieces of equipment which connect to a number of monitors. Here the monitors are often suspended from the ceiling.

Other activities in which a simple single camera chain may be used with educational advantage are for practice in film-making techniques, as a way of presenting project material, for spoken English exercises and for liberal studies work.

A second camera opens up entirely new production opportunities and enables studio-type lessons to be presented. It also calls for the employment of a team of people consisting of, *at least*, a producer, floor manager, two camera operators and a presenter. The equipment too becomes more

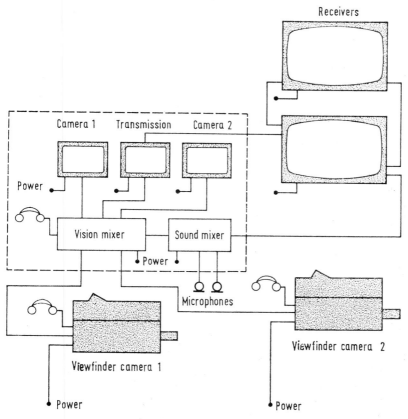

FIG. 98. The start of a television studio

complex. The cameras must work in synchronism; if they do not, when the producer switches from one to the other the picture will roll up or down the screen before the new one becomes fixed, and this calls for synchronizing equipment. The producer will need to see what each camera is shooting and what picture he is transmitting, and therefore he needs three monitors. He will need to speak to the operators and the floor manager and this means a sound link for the purpose. Naturally equipment of this complexity must be selected with forethought and understanding (*Fig.* 98) and must be seen as

163

quite different in its implications from single camera episcope substitutes. It must be realized too that once the equipment is installed its users will press heavily for more—for a caption camera, a tape recorder, a record player, for telecine, a studio, for more lights, more assistants, more . . . and this calls for some serious cost analysis *before* a second television camera is bought.

CLASS OBSERVATION

Closed circuit television employing more than one camera can be used with a measure of success in certain teacher-training activities and in particular for observing classes and teachers at work. The use of television for this purpose reduces the observation time which trainees need to spend in schools and also makes it possible to give more efficient guidance in observation of classroom behaviour. This unobserved viewing enables groups to discuss what they see whilst they are seeing it and because each group member sees the same aspect of the lesson it can lead to closely-knit discussions of relevant issues.

Three methods are used for this work—each with its merits. The first is to bring the class and its teacher to the college which is fitted with house closed circuit television and for the lessons to be given in a room which has previously been prepared for this purpose. Under these circumstances the technical provision can be excellent but the environment and the circumstances in which the children are taught is artificial. A second method is to connect the cameras in a school classroom to monitors in the college through cables rented from the GPO for this purpose. This presents the camera operators with the technical difficulties of "working away from home," is comparatively expensive and inflexible but it leaves the class in its accustomed surroundings. A third method is to video tape the lesson for subsequent viewing. This is efficient in that tapes can be previewed and only suitable lessons need be shown, or parts of lessons can be selected for viewing, but the excitement of immediacy is reduced. Of course, tapes can be stored and used over and over again. The ILEA has elected to extend its use of the third technique using a permanent team of experts to prepare the tapes. *Fig.* 99 shows a television vehicle suitable for televising away from base.

Since lessons cannot be rehearsed and since classrooms are almost invariably the most unpromising of studios, the human and technical problems which the television director must face are daunting. Yet remarkable successes have been achieved. Opinions on the most suitable techniques vary but some general conclusions have been reached. For instance, children and students do become almost indifferent to the television equipment and operators in the fairly short time of about an hour or so. This means that one dummy run is usually sufficient participant preparation.

164

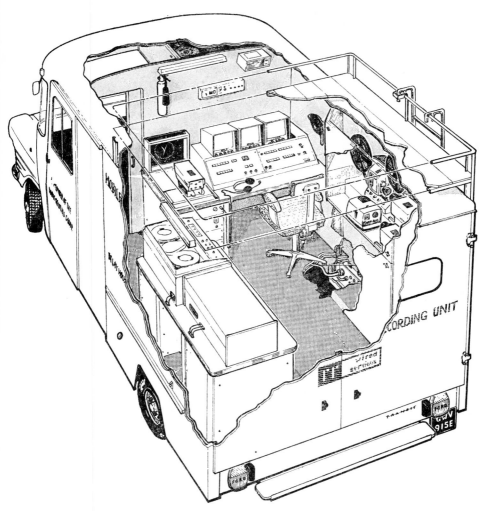

FIG. 99.   A television recording van
(*By permission RR Wired Services Ltd.*)

SOME TECHNICAL NOTES

Sound presents the greatest problem. Rooms can be improved acoustically by using sound-absorbent display surfaces and curtains, but naturally, these should be fixed well before the day chosen for the shooting. (From the engineer's point of view a really untidy room with children's coats and other impedimenta strewn around would be fine!) Tony Gibson of Goldsmiths' College, who has developed a remarkable "one man" shooting technique, uses three or four clusters of high impedance crystal microphones which plug into junction boxes in a multicore cable and are hung or taped to the most promising parts of the room. There are up to twenty-four of them in all and any one can be selected by means of a press button.

Another favoured method is for the producer to walk around the room holding a portable moving-coil microphone near to each centre of interest in turn and for the teacher to wear a halter microphone or, better still, to carry a radio microphone. Yet another is to use a microphone with a parabolic reflector and so on.

There is no doubt that a surprising standard of flexibility of production is achieved when the entire job is left to a well-trained and well-briefed camera operator. He controls his own camera, can switch to a fixed, general-view camera, possibly to a third remotely-controlled camera and he controls the sound switching. There is also no doubt that two camera operators and a producer working with a teacher in a classroom can produce technically better television. But whatever method is used, the work calls for particular combinations of personal qualities and abilities and the remarkable results which are being produced reflect, not only the effectiveness of the medium, but the remarkable people producing them.

Naturally, the technical and production aspects of this work cannot be understood without training but certain facts should be generally known. An untrained presenter has no sense of time in the absence of a class and this can cause difficulties. Furthermore, television lessons are so concentrated and so "reliable" that pauses must be built into them: this the untrained presenter generally fails to do. The total labour cost of producing a twenty-minute studio lesson under college conditions is usually sufficient to employ one teacher full-time for half a term.

Closed circuit television signals can be transmitted as video signals or as video signals superimposed on a radio-frequency signal. The former give a better picture over short distances but need special monitors or modified receivers to display them. Radio-frequency signals on the other hand can be used for long runs and work with ordinary domestic receivers: the quality of the picture they produce, however, is lower. With radio-frequency transmission, amplification is straightforward and the coaxial cables will carry more than one signal and the sound as well, but although in video transmission only one video signal can be transmitted by each cable it is less prone to interference. So again, advice should be sought.

166

Within a classroom the receiver screen should be so placed that it is not obscured for any students by reflections from windows or lights. It can be well above floor level provided the maximum vertical viewing angle does not exceed about 30°. A 23-in. screen, in general, is the most suitable size for classroom use as pictures on larger screens lack definition.

REFERENCES

1. SCUPHAM, JOHN, *E.T.V. East and West: Japan and Britain, A Survey*, Published by the British Film Institute, 1967.
2. BARRINGTON, H., A Survey of Instructional Television Researches, *Educational Research*, **8**, 1, pp. 8–25, 1965.
3. WHITE, HARVEY E., More Effective Teaching of Physics through Television, *American Journal of Physics*, 28, 368, 1960.
4. MACFARLANE-SMITH, I., An Experimental Study of the Effect of Television Broadcasts on the G Courses in Engineering Science, *The Vocational Aspect*, **17**, 37, pp. 87–177, 1965.

FURTHER READING

BBC, *Educational Television and Radio in Britain—a new Phase in Education*, 1966.
COSTELLO, L. and GORDEN, G. N., *Teaching with Television*, New York, Hastings House, 1961.
DAVIS, DESMOND, *The Grammar of Television Production*, London, Barrie & Rockliff, 1965.
JONES, PETER, *The Techniques of the T.V. Camerman*, Focal Press, 1965.
MILLERSON, GERALD, *Techniques of Television Production*, 4th ed., London, Focal Press, 1966.
NATIONAL COMMITTEE FOR AUDIO VISUAL AIDS IN EDUCATION, *Report 2. Closed Circuit Television in Education in Great Britain, Experimental Development Unit*, 1965.
SPEAR, J., *Creating Visuals for T.V.*, National Education Association, 1962.

9 PROGRAMMED LEARNING

Programmed instruction seems to be one of those activities that people are willing to play around with for a long time but never come to grips with. In some cases it may well turn out to be an eternal experiment.
Programmed Instruction in BEA, W. S. BARRY, Pergamon, 1967.

A programme is a coherent body of knowledge presented in such a fashion that, in the absence of a teacher, a learner for whom it is intended will want to learn it and will be successful in doing so. Generally it consists of a sequence of rather small instructional steps followed by questions to which the learner gives a sufficient number of correct answers to feel motivated to continue: it exploits the process of differential reinforcement.

Teaching machines are devices for presenting these programmes in such a manner as to relieve the learner of tactical decision making. Programmed learning is an educational development with many roots. One leads out to the tutorial system in which one tutor teaches one student by questioning, listening, explaining and correcting in such a way as to match the pressure of teaching demand as precisely as possible to the knowledge and learning abilities of the student at the moment, as implied by his frequent responses. The tutorial system has a very long history of success. At its best it teaches a student how to learn. Another root reaches out into the popular teach-yourself literature which, together with correspondence courses also has a long tradition of commercial success. Many adult students would like to learn but are reluctant to do so too publicly. Very many evening students enrol for preliminary courses in pairs rather than as individuals for the same basic reason: they lack the self-confidence to face the prospect of public failure without the support of a friend. And, to a very large extent, programmed learning satisfies this preference for keeping one's limitations to oneself and attracts those who, indeed, want to learn, but are inhibited from doing so when they contemplate the social environment in which it will take place. Yet other roots reach out to the work of psychologists.

E. L. Thorndike at the beginning of the century concluded that a learner should not progress to a second step until he had understood the first one.

LINEAR PROGRAMMES

B. F. Skinner of Harvard, consequent upon researches with animals and birds, concluded that learning should be broken down into very small steps so that when, after each step, the learner was required to express what he had learned, at least ninety-five per cent of his responses would be correct and also that he should know immediately upon responding whether he was right or not. This is the stimulus—response—reinforcement sequence of operant conditioning and forms the basis of what is known as linear programming (*Fig.* 100).

Linear programme

FIG. 100. Pattern of a linear programme

In such a programme each of the learning steps is called a frame. Since the learner "writes in" his answer it is referred to as a constructed response which, according to Skinner elicits deeper thinking and greater motivation than would a more mechanical response. The basic form of a linear programme is given on page 170.

This sequence is aiming towards a clearly defined and limited objective—an understanding of the concept of e.m.f. and the definition of an e.m.f. of one volt as a joule per coulomb. It has a certain group of students in mind who have a knowledge of work and energy and the basic M.K.S. units in mechanics. Notice that the responses which are constructed are keys to understanding, that they are repeated, that each step overlaps its neighbours and that there are prompts to the correct response—the word an, for example, must be followed by a vowel and the space available after it invites a long word.

A most important characteristic of this type of programme is that each response is an integral part of the process of learning.

BRANCHING PROGRAMMES

Norman Crowder of US Industries reached a similar conclusion but one which gives rise to a different kind of presentation. He found that the immediate external reinforcement of each small step was unnecessary and, indeed, detrimental to efficiency in many areas of learning because it frustrated the abler learner. He held that reinforcement occurred as the learning unfolded—it was intrinsic to the experience of learning. Consequently he concluded that knowledge should be presented in small but coherent and

169

Frame	Stimulus	Response
1	Any device which drives current around a circuit is called an electricity generator. A dry battery and a running dynamo are electricity.................................	generators
2	An electromotive force will drive current around a circuit and consequently there is an............................ in an electricity generator	electromotive force
3	An .... in a dry battery drives current around a circuit	electromotive force
4	When a dynamo is running it generates an...........................	electromotive force
5	Chemical energy in a battery is used up in circulating a current around a circuit. The electromotive force (e.m.f.) is obtained at the expense of chemical............................	energy
6	In a dynamo, the e.m.f. is obtained at the expense of mechanical	energy

complete steps after which the learner should be asked a question. Now since he has attempted to learn not just one, but a related group of ideas, the test questions must discover not only whether he has been successful but, if he has not, why he has failed. Consequently multiple choice questions are generally set and so selected as to indicate where the learner's *thinking* was wrong if he gives an incorrect response. Giving an incorrect response then automatically directs him to learn the same group of ideas again but this time in such a way as to overcome the difficulty he evidently experienced. This type of programme is called an intrinsic or branching programme: it is suitable for a wider variety of learning abilities. The basic form of a branching programme is given in *Fig.* 101; an example is given on p. 171.

Along with programmes, machines and devices were developed for presenting them. An early machine which was designed by Pressey of Ohio presented information on a sequence of cards. Each card would move on to reveal the next one only when the learner pressed a key corresponding to the right answer. By the 1960s Gordon Pask had built machines that automatically adjusted the sequence of information and demand to accommodate to the learner's mode of learning. The best known is probably the SAKI Keyboard Trainer for teaching punched card work.

Frame	Stimulus	Response
1	A dry battery, and a dynamo whilst it is running, are electric generators. Both will drive current around a circuit and, whilst current is flowing, energy conversion takes place in the generator. In a dry battery chemical energy is being changed into electrical energy whilst, in a dynamo, mechanical energy is used up. The measure of the electrical driving force in a generator is called its electromotive force. The electromotive force in a battery is derived from:	
	(a) the electric current which is circulating around the circuit	Press button A
	(b) the chemicals from which the battery is made	Press button B
	(c) another generator such as a dynamo	Press button C

PRESSING BUTTON A REVEALS THE FOLLOWING FRAME:

Frame	Stimulus	Response
1 *(a)*	The current which circulates around a circuit is caused by the electromotive force. If the battery were disconnected and the battery leads then joined together no current would flow because there is nothing in the circuit to drive it. Press the RETURN button and read frame 1 again	Press RETURN

PRESSING BUTTON B REVEALS THE FOLLOWING FRAME:

Frame	Stimulus	Response
2	Your answer is correct. The electromotive force of a battery can drive a small current around the circuit for a long time before the battery is "used up" but it becomes exhausted much sooner if the current is a large one. If an electromotive force drives 12 coulombs around a circuit at a steady rate in 6 seconds, the current which flows is $$\frac{12 \text{ coulombs}}{6 \text{ seconds}} = 2 \text{ C/s}$$ $$= 2 \text{ amperes (2 A)}$$ If a current of 5 A flows for 10 minutes, the total charge moved by the electromotive force is:	
	(a) 3,000 coulombs	Press button A
	(b) 120 coulombs	Press button B
	(c) 50 coulombs	Press button C

PRESSING BUTTON C REVEALS THE FOLLOWING FRAME:

Frame	Stimulus	Response
1 *(c)*	A dry battery is an electric generator. In an electric torch it will drive current through a lamp and light it. No other generator is needed. This electric current is circulated by the battery; if the battery is removed and its leads joined together no current will flow. Press the RETURN button and read frame 1 again.	Press RETURN

Once machines—particularly the Auto Tutor made by US Industries Inc. and the Grundytutor made by International Tutor Machines Ltd.—became known, cheaper alternative presentation devices were sought and marketed; some driven electrically, some mechanically, and some hand-operated; some with the programme on film, some on cards, and some on paper. The scope of machines was widened to accommodate other prepared material: slides, filmstrips, tape recordings, science equipment and so on. And with this spate of material came programmed textbooks, some in linear form, where the learner works through consecutive pages and some, in branching form, where the learner, having selected his answer from a multiple choice,

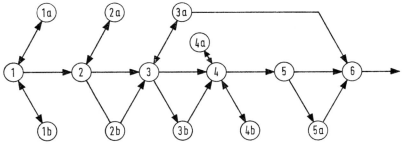

Branching programme

FIG. 101. Pattern of a branching programme

is told which page he must read next. The latter are sometimes called scrambled texts.

The proof of any programme lies, not in the extent to which it is supported by a theoretical model of the learning process, but the efficiency of the learning to which it gives rise. And as we have seen in earlier chapters this embraces the changes in attitudes towards learning which the technique may engender.

ADJUNCTIVE PROGRAMMES

One new form of programme has emerged from the experimentation as particularly successful in many areas of learning, namely the adjunctive-type programme. This looks rather like the short chapters of a book, each chapter containing a coherent, interconnected and interdependent group of facts and concepts. The chapters are broken down into paragraphs but these have been built from carefully selected components of knowledge in the same way as the steps are selected for a branching programme. The learner reads the whole chapter before he is tested and then answers, what seems to be, an objective-type test paper: this is the adjunctive section of the programme. If he is correct in all of his answers he goes on to the next chapter; if not, he is referred back to a particular paragraph which corresponds to the stage at which his understanding broke down. This type of programme directs the learner's attention to the cognitive aspects of reading and the training it provides transfers to the reading for meaning of conventional books.

From a utilitarian point of view the adjunctive-type programme can more easily open up wide opportunities for learning by directing learners to practical work and investigations of various kinds: it has both a flexibility which is in keeping with our intuitive ideas about education and a rigour which satisfies the principles which emerge from learning experiments.

On the face of it, linear programming might seem the most suitable sequence for teaching facts, techniques and skills of a routine and repetitive kind, branching programmes for teaching concepts and adjunctive programmes for problem solving, decision taking and management skills generally, but it is of the nature of the exercise that we must FIND OUT.

The considerable body of research into programmed learning suggests the following conclusions but these are still very much open to correction and local variation and to the effects of changes in attitude towards the method which will arise as it becomes more widely used:

1. Linear programmes seem most suitable for teaching facts, techniques and simple skills to operatives and craftsmen or to those school learners who are of average or below average ability.
2. Adjunctive programmes seem more suitable for teaching problem-solving techniques.

Much research leads to the conclusion that programmed learning can save up to fifty per cent of training time in certain areas of industrial training.

Because of the growing body of information, specific references to research are not included but the interested reader is recommended to keep in touch with, for example, the Association for Programmed Learning, the National Centre for Programmed Learning at Birmingham University, or BACIE.

It is not the purpose here to show how to write programmes; this has been well described in a number of books and is best developed by attending a course. However, the principles behind doing so are relevant.

PREPARING OBJECTIVES

Before writing a programme it is essential to define the learners for whom the programme is to be prepared and to make a precise statement of what the learner will be able to DO when he has worked through it: in other words to state the objectives of the programme in behavioural terms. Such statements as, "The student will understand the binary system" or, "He will be able to drive a car well," are not suitable since they give no exact indication of how well the student will know or perform these tasks.

In behavioural terms the objectives of the first might be stated thus:

173

The programme is to be designed for any person who has passed O-level mathematics at any grade within the last six years. On completion he will:

1. be able to write correctly in binary notation any number up to 64 within fifteen seconds of being asked to do so.
2. be able to convert thirty different numbers reasonably distributed between zero and 100,000 in less than half an hour to binary notation making fewer than three errors.
3. be able to add and subtract any two numbers reasonably distributed between zero and 100,000 written in binary notation, making fewer than three errors in thirty attempts in less than twenty minutes.
4. be able to convert ten numbers reasonably distributed between zero and 100,000 from binary notation to decimal notation making fewer than three errors in less than five minutes.

Against this statement, the terminal test to be used at the end of the programme can be written. The next stage consists of writing down all of the steps which must be learned in order to achieve the standard of responding which is required. Here all relevant material is included and, as important, all unnecessary material excluded, although some may be brought back into the frames to provide for a fluent sequence of repetition. Thus, in the terminal requirements of the binary programme no mention is made of the word "computer" and consequently it will not appear in the steps. Notice that in a conventional lesson fringe information is almost inevitably included.

After this the programme itself is constructed by following certain technical rules that have become established. The programme is then tried out on a few people who fit into the categories for which it was designed and their progress is observed very closely so that the programme can be revised in the light of their responses. This revision continues until the programme seems to meet the requirements of its objectives, after which it is given a preliminary field trial under the control of a typical user. This—or these— provide the final ammendments which make the programme ready for everyday use, and in this final form they may seem somewhat different from the examples given earlier. On page 175 is an extract from a linear programme designed for use with a Grundymaster machine—the plates to which it refers are omitted. It should be read from the bottom upwards since the sheets move downwards past the viewing window as the programme is used.

An extract from a branching programme for use on a machine is given on pages 177–82. The flow chart of this sequence is shown in *Fig*. 102. (Note that the letters A, B, C, etc., at the end of each frame refer to the push-buttons on the machine.) Both programme extracts are reproduced by kind permission of International Tutor Machines Ltd.

18. We set the stroke length when the Ram is about to move forward for the cutting stroke. Look at the machine; you will see a clutch lever marked (B) in Plate 3. By moving this lever into the position marked IN, we can move the Ram backwards and forwards over its full stroke.

Turn on

17. The stroke length if measured from the position the Ram reaches at the end of its return stroke to its extreme forward position on the forward stroke.

Look at Plate 3; what letter marks the Stroke Adjustment Shaft?

A

16. If our stroke length is at least 12in. the Ram (will/will not) push the cutting tool over the whole of length x in Plate 2.

will

15. We have to make a cut that is 12in. long, therefore we have to turn shaft (A) (Plate 3) so that our _____ length is at least 12in.

stroke

14. Before we can turn the Stroke Adjustment Shaft marked _____ (Plate 3) we must untighten a L____ N____ .

A
Lock Nut

13. If you look on the body of the machine you will see a scale in inches. When we turn the shaft (A) (Plate 3) we move the Ram along this scale until a pointer shows us we have the stroke length we want. In the diagram the stroke length has been set at   .
What is the longest stroke we could set on the scale shown?

12in.

18in.

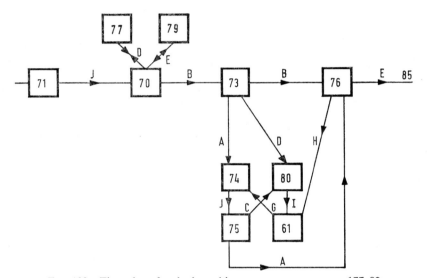

FIG. 102. Flow chart for the branching programme on pages 177–82

The fundamental aim of Network Analysis is to minimize the duration and/or cost of a project.

This is achieved by identifying the "critical" path of activities and concentrating resources on these activities. The thick line in this network is the critical path.

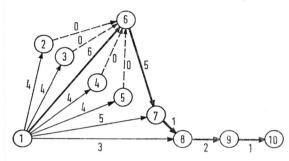

What is the duration of this critical path?

15 hours

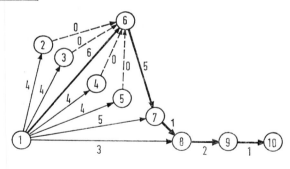

The critical path is the _____ of all the paths through the network. (Be careful about this one.)

longest   B
shortest   E
average   D

79

No. At first thought one might well expect the critical path to be the shortest in duration, but this is not so. The critical activities are the ones which threaten to cause delays, and are therefore the ones on which resources are to be concentrated. See if you can find a path in this network which has a duration longer than 15 hours.

RETURN

77

No, not the average.

The critical activities are the ones which threaten to cause delays, and are therefore the ones on which resources are to be concentrated.

See if you can find a path in this network which has a duration longer than 15 hours.

RETURN

Yes, the critical path is the longest. There is no other path with a duration as long as 15 hours.

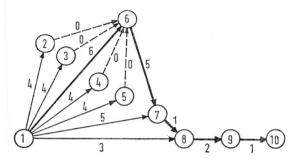

This brings us to one definition of the critical path. It is the path of longest duration, and therefore the one which controls the duration of the project as a whole. By the "duration" of the project we mean simply the period between the moment it starts and the moment it finishes, not, for example, the total of man-hours spent on the project. The duration of this project is 15 hours.

If the duration of the critical path is increased by 1 hour, the duration of the project is increased by 1 hour. Similarly if the duration of any activity on the critical path is increased, the duration of the project is increased by a corresponding amount.

If the duration of activity 1, 7 on the path 1, 7, 8, 9, 10 is increased by one hour, what difference does this make to the duration of the project?

Increases it	*A*
Decreases it	*D*
Makes no difference	*B*

No. The duration of the project would not be increased. The duration of the project, on the present estimates, is 15 hours.

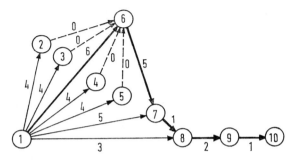

What is the duration of the path 1, 7, 8, 9, 10?

J

75

The path 1, 7, 8, 9, 10 has a duration of 9 hours. We know that the critical path has a duration of 15 hours.

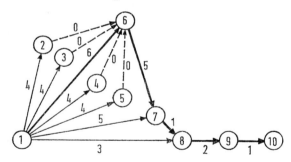

If the duration of activity 1, 7 is increased by 1 hour the duration of path 1, 7, 8, 9, 10 is increased by 1 hour.

What effect does this have on the duration of the whole project?

Decreases it   C

Makes no difference   A

No. The duration of the project would not be decreased. The duration of the project is determined by the duration of the longest path (critical path) in the project. This on the present estimates is 15 hours.

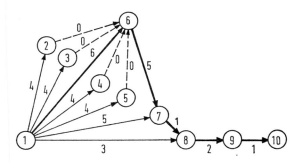

What is the duration of the path 1, 7, 8, 9, 10?

I

The duration of the path 1, 7, 8, 9, 10 is <u>9 hours.</u>

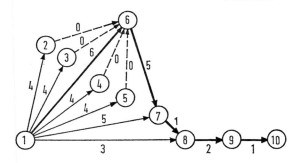

If the duration of activity 1, 7 is increased by 1 hour, the duration of path 1, 7, 8, 9, 10 is increased by 1 hour.

What effect does this have on the duration of the whole project?

Increases it   *G*

Makes no difference   *H*

181

Good. The duration of the project is not affected at all by an increase of one hour in the duration of activity 1, 7. This is because activity 1, 7 is on the path 1, 7, 8, 9, 10, which is not the critical path.

SUMMARY

You have now seen the stages of Network Analysis up to the point of finding the critical path. The stages are:

1. Break down the project into a sequence of constituent activities, and estimate the durations.
2. Put these activities on to an arrow diagram to show how they are interrelated.
3. Identify the critical path.

This is the end of Part 1. In Part 2 you will be constructing some networks.

When you are ready for Part 2, press *E*.

This rather sketchy outline shows the process which leads to the production of a teaching programme and indicates, by implication, why programmes are successful. Until they are of such a form as to do what they are designed to do they are incomplete and not ready for publication. Unfortunately, many so-called programmes are not subjected to the rigorous validation procedures which alone can fashion real programmes and, as a consequence, the real ones may be rejected because of the reputation garnered by the fakes.

The growing use of programmed instruction in industry is brought out in a survey conducted in 1966 by Romiszowski.[1] He concludes that "programmed learning has not only been accepted as a powerful industrial training method, but that its use will continue to grow both in quantity and in variety of application."

REFERENCES

1. ROMISZOWSKI, A. J., A Survey of the use of Programmed Learning in Industry during 1966, *Programmed Learning News*, Vol. 1, No. 3, 1967.

FURTHER READING

BBC, *What is Programmed Learning?* London, 1965, 104 pp.
BACIE, *Register of Programmed Instruction in the Field of Education and Training in Commerce and Industry*, London, 1966, 40 pp. and Vol. 2, 1968, 190 pp.
BARRY, W. S., *Programmed Instruction in BEA*, London, Pergamon Press, 1967, 46 pp.
BRETHOWER, DALE, M., *Programed Instruction: a Manual of Programing Techniques*, London, Pitman, 1963, 268 pp. (In the form of a programme.)
BRITISH IRON AND STEEL FEDERATION, *Programmed Instruction: a report issued by the Training Department*, London, BISF, 1965.
DAVEY, D. MACKENZIE, and MCDONNELL, P., *Programmed Instruction*, London, Institute of Personnel Management, 1964, 56 pp.
HALL, C, and FLETCHER, R. N., *Programmed Techniques in the GPO*, London, Pergamon Press, 1967.
HOLLAND, JAMES G. and SKINNER, B. F., *The Analysis of Behavior*, New York, McGraw-Hill, 1961, 337 pp.
JEFFELS, A., *Basic Workshop Training for ICT Engineering Apprentices*, London, Pergamon Press, 1967.
KAY, H. et al., *Teaching Machines and their use in Industry*, H.M.S.O. (Department of Scientific and Industrial Research—Problems in Industry 14), London, 1963, 32 pp.
MARKLE, SUSAN MEYER, *Good Frames and Bad: a Grammar of Frame Writing*, New York, Wiley, 1964, 278 pp.
MARKLE, SUSAN MEYER, et al., *A Programmed Primer on Programming*, New York, Centre for Programmed Instruction, 1961, 343 frames.
NATIONAL COMMITTEE FOR AUDIO-VISUAL AIDS IN EDUCATION, *Programmed Learning*, London, 1966.
ROWNTREE, DEREK, *Basically Branching*, London, Macdonald, 1966.
THOMAS, C. A., DAVIES, I. K., OPPENSHAW, D. and BIRD, J. B., *Programmed Learning in Perspective: A Guide to Programme Writing*, London, City Publicity Services, 1963, 182 pp.

THE ENVIRONMENT

10 TEAM TEACHING

There is something imperfect about shutting a teacher in a room with a group of learners every day of every week for a whole course. If the teacher is very competent the learners are fortunate but the teacher never experiences the kind of encouragement that an adult can get from another qualified adult. If the teacher is just competent the learners are unfortunate and the teacher never gets help or, if he needs it, criticism from his peers. We all need this kind of publicity: its lack can produce the personality defects that, alas, are not sufficiently uncommon: head-teachers who talk down to parents, insult children and assume the roles of arbitrary dictators of fashion, manners and organization, teachers who are too timid to face adult appraisal or to talk to head-teachers as man to man, tired teachers who have wearied for want of a friendly companion during teaching time and so on. These personality failures may not begin with teaching but they are undoubtedly nurtured by it: the distribution curves of human qualities sit as inexorably on teachers as they do on any other large group of people.

Furthermore there is something imperfect about, for example, the quality of laboratory reporting being "nothing to do with English" or the accuracy of workshop processes being "nothing to do with mathematics" or the Industrial Revolution being mulled over first as history and then as geography and then as economics and town planning and art and social studies—each nibbling its special titbit off the body of the thing.

Furthermore it seems a pity that the film on, say, "Day and Night" cannot be seen by the geography class because it is being used by a mathematics class and in any case the only other projector is being used to show a science class how the planets move relative to the sun.

It is sad if the one or two children with spelling difficulties cannot be taken aside regularly and given the sympathetic professional help which teachers are trained to give.

Thoughts like these lie behind the development of team teaching in which closely co-operating groups of teachers, with or without other assistance, are jointly responsible for the education of groups of learners. Recently these ideas have been more precisely formulated and foremost amongst them is the

184

belief that the size of a learning group should, as far as possible, depend upon the learning experience for which it is assembled. Thus a trainee who, alone among his fellows, is unable to convert fractions to decimals would best be taught alone, whilst a group brought together to hear a symphony as part of a musical appreciation course could number hundreds. The different special communications competencies of teachers, it is argued, should be more efficiently exploited: the experienced and very able teachers should be in a position to influence and guide the inexperienced and less able, the brilliant teacher should have opportunities for teaching more often whilst good tutors who do less well in classrooms should exploit their talents appropriately, and so on.

To assist with this reallocation, work which calls for non-teaching abilities such as the maintenance and use of equipment, the preparation of teaching aids, and certain kinds of training should be in the hands of non-teaching staff. Also the timetable module should be smaller to permit of greater variety in period length than is conventional.

And, of course, there are the pragmatists who, quite properly, point out that professional recognition will come only when teachers are supported in their work by able and responsible groups of non-teachers: do-it-yourself, they say, is a game played by amateurs.

However, team teaching appears to be unsuitable for some teachers and for some learners. Its success depends upon an agreement in general terms on the functions of education and on the roles of teachers, and some teachers are unable to accept the loss of autonomy which the arrangement implies. Some learners are bewildered by the more dynamic nature of the learning environment and are made unhappy by losing the greater sense of security which habit provides.

But where team teaching has developed, lessons seem to have been prepared more thoroughly and more thoughtfully, students have matured in their self-discipline and ability to work unsupervised and timetables have become more flexible. As one student remarked, "Both teaching and learning have become professional occupations." It is evident too, that many teachers who have participated in team teaching, experience a new sense of excitement, of security and—what for want of a better word might be called—normality. Subjects, they report, lose their unreal independence and equipment can be more widely shared and more professionally utilized. In evaluating its progress so far, we should keep in mind one important factor: almost all teachers have been professionally trained for solo performances and in this they are at present supported by the tradition and experience behind them. This development, therefore, is breaking difficult new ground and if it is only as successful as the arrangement it replaces, it is successful.

ORGANIZATION

The actual pattern of team teaching varies widely since, to a large extent, it develops from the needs of the students as these become revealed. One of many arrangements consists of a group of five people responsible for sixty students and structured as follows:

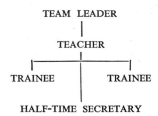

Here, the responsibility for the work rests finally with the team leader. He is chosen for his professional experience and ability in teaching. The student-teacher ratio is actually 30:1 but the student-adult ratio 15:1, or lower depending upon the kind of work undertaken by the part-time secretary.

The advantages that could lie with such a group are:

1. All students and adults profit from the greater professional competency of the team leader.
2. All students and adults profit from the fresh knowledge and less conditioned approaches of the trainees.
3. The total team responsibility is greater than could be that of a single class teacher and this sense of responsibility is shared.
4. The values of small group relationships which are essential to a natural social environment are enjoyed by the team members.
5. Ability to teach is recognized without promoting the teacher to a post involving less teaching.
6. Secretarial assistance is available as of right.
7. Preparation can be shared to accommodate special abilities and preferences.
8. More material and equipment can be available to the group than to its members individually.
9. Individual help and seminar work can be more effectively shared.

The University of Winsconsin, reporting on the value of such team work as early as the years 1961–2 and 1962–3 concluded: "First-grade-level team pupils were significantly ahead of self-contained first-graders on achievement tests, and second-grade-level team pupils were significantly above the second-grade self-contained class in language." In no areas did the differences favour self-contained classes.

If there is no improvement in attainment but greater social harmony either for students or teachers or both, then unless there is some other factor to outweigh this advantage the method has value.

THE HENBURY FINDINGS

In England, team teaching has developed in this and other ways. One favoured alternative is to begin team teaching within a subject department. For example, this method was employed by the history department of the Henbury School, Bristol—a nine-form entry school, but its success during 1963–4 led to co-operation with the geography and religious knowledge departments. For want of a better title, since the combined subject was concerned with man in his environment, the combined subjects were renamed "Humanity." The method used there consists of opening each new learning phase with a "key" or "lead" lesson followed by consolidation and activity lessons. The key lesson is presented through very carefully prepared audio-visuals: a tape recording suitably supported by film, slides, or film strips, and lasting a total time of about sixteen minutes. The course began with the geographers taking the lead for six weeks followed by the historians for the rest of the term and so on. The religious knowledge teacher related the main themes to his specialism. Every development was carefully geared to the needs, interests and abilities of the learners: nothing was included simply because it always had been, nothing was omitted because it was new or organizationally awkward. One result of this learner-centred learning was more activity in the form of field studies and investigations, a breaking down of the conventional classroom and timetable divisions, greater involvement of non-teachers, project work, enormous enthusiasm and a great deal of rethinking of content. The course has been further developed and modified in recent years.

House studio presentations by closed circuit television are a form of team teaching but to derive the kind of total involvement represented by the Henbury results, the full teaching team must include the teachers who are with the students at the receiver as well as those who actually work in the studio.

KEY LESSONS

Training for key lesson presentation, whether intended for team teaching or for television is given in Garnett College to groups of students consisting of specialists in Nautical Subjects, Printing Subjects, Physics, Mathematics, Chemistry and Biology. Here again, the titles of the presentations cut across subject barriers—"The Moon," "Position Finding," "Famine," and so on, and their form and content are exciting educative springboards.

For example, the team which presented the key lesson "Famine" consisted of twelve men and women, the class contained about 240 students and the

187

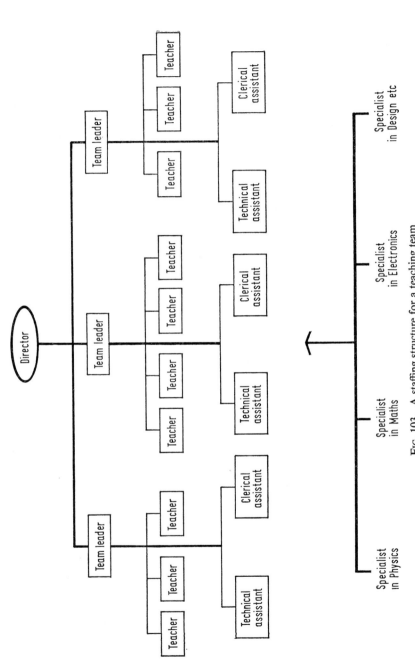

Fig. 103. A staffing structure for a teaching team

lesson lasted about fifty minutes. The team responsibilities divided roughly as follows:

Team leader
Management and control of technical equipment
Preparation of aids
Research into (a) Population growth
           (b) Social and religious aspects
           (c) Land utilization and reclamation
           (d) Nutrition and synthetic foods
           (e) Sea farming
           (f) Attitudes towards birth control

The lesson opened with a folk song, "Two Little Fishes" being faded out as one presenter read a part of the Parable of the Loaves and Fishes. This led to the statement of the problem first in statistical terms by means of a series of overhead projector transparencies and then in human terms by a snatch of film. This opening lasted only a few minutes and it is this economical use of time and this capacity for presenting a few ideas with tremendous force that can make key lessons the power source which will sustain tutorials, classwork and private study.

There are schools and colleges where the patterns of social relationships are medieval. Fully developed team teaching *could* lead to a more open staffing structure and an end to this anachronism (*Fig.* 103).

Perhaps team teaching is a technique with a future: perhaps not. But since educational change has been dammed for so long it is breaking free in a revolution: a revolution with its false starts, its setbacks and its premature victories. But these are all part of the small cost of the new vitality of mind and the new freedom of spirit that we believe can be the birthright of the people of tomorrow.

FURTHER READING

BLAIR, M. and WOODWARD, R. G., *Team Teaching in Action*, New York, Houghton Mifflin, 1964.
FORD FOUNDATION, *Better Utilization of College Teaching Resources*, New York, 1959.
LOVELL, K., *Team Teaching*, University of Leeds Institute of Education, 1967.
SHAPLIN, J. T. and OLDS, H. F., *Team Teaching*, New York, Harper & Row, 1964.
MANSELL, JACK, Team Teaching and Conditions of Service, *The Technical Journal*, Oct. 1967, pp. 8–9.
RICHMOND, W. KENNETH, *The Teaching Revolution*, London, Methuen, 1967.
VAIZEY, JOHN, *Education in the Modern World*, World University Library, London, Weidenfeld & Nicolson, 1967.

11 PLANNING FOR LEARNING

The new devices and materials which are being introduced into schools, colleges and industry, are important, not so much for the individual contributions they can make to the learning process as for the impact they are having upon the whole field of educational thought and practice. Unlike schools of the past which were built and equipped for teachers to teach in, schools of the present and future will be built and equipped for learners to learn in. And instead of a learner's hope of success in a particular subject being inextricably bound to the competency and personality of one subject teacher, it will now be shared with groups of teachers who can advise and teach, and with unseen experts in subject matter and in the theory of learning. Often the student will work with other learners whom he has chosen as companions rather than with classmates provided for him by the organizational demands of a classroom orientated timetable.

LEARNER-CENTRED EDUCATION

Learner-centred education is not new. There have been the works and practices of great educationists and there have been the brave lone practitioners; there have also been the unrecorded hundreds who have risked censure and reaped love by their submission to the true purpose of their vocation. But now there is too much evidence pointing to the greater value of planning for learning rather than for teaching, there are too many good alternatives to the badly taught classroom lesson or lecture, there is too much publicity and too few teachers to hold back the learning revolution.

When the classroom was the focal point and the teacher gave information, the successful student was the well informed one, but today, being well informed is not, in itself, enough even if we could decide what well informed means in a world which spawns information at an ever increasing rate.

And so it is too with the directed learning that occurs during earning—what, for want of a more descriptive word—is called, training. When, in order to earn, most folk learned to do what more experienced workers were already doing, the process was one of imitation, but today this would lead to economic stagnation. Both in education and in training we must continuously

190

question both the object of the process and the process itself. And in both phases one priority is for intellectual resilience: in education for providing a climate in which the best human qualities have the greatest opportunity to develop, and in training to provide learners with the most direct means of fulfilling their needs through work. These are vague value statements which can be given form and meaning only through philosophy, but in the context of this work they must suffice. We are concerned with the effects of the reappraisals.

RESOURCES CENTRES

If buildings are designed to be learned in, they must accommodate:
1. Those who come to learn
2. The sources from which they learn
3. Those who maintain the sources and sustain the learners

Conventionally, these would be students, teachers and aids, technicians, librarians and caterers; but the conventional divisions of the past are already ill defined. Teachers must quite often be students, technicians undoubtedly teach and if we are to think in terms of places to learn in, we cease to be sensitive about who does what as long as it is well done. The process which is common to the whole activity in a college or training school is communication of a kind that presents learners with selected difficulties: the building should be designed and maintained in such a way as to remove as far as possible all other difficulties whether they be physical or psychological ones. But for an educationist to state his requirements and then abdicate all responsibility, until he criticizes the finished building, is irresponsible: only if architects, engineers, and educationists co-operatively create the inevitable compromises, can the work be successful. The rest of this chapter is intended to provide educationists with a glimpse of the ideas and adjustments with which they should be involved.

The core of a learning place might well be the learning and resources centre where information would be stored in such forms as would make it most easily accessible for learning. It would include a book, film, video tape, transparency and audio-record library with all sources classified, and also a repository of the devices designed to make this information available.

It would probably be convenient to separate the information-handling centre from the equipment store, so that technical maintenance would cause less interference with learning. Then the library centre would issue books, tapes, records, programmes, loop films, films and transparencies which would be used, either for private study in the library area or elsewhere. Provision for private study with book-type materials, could be met as now by tables and chairs within the library itself, while materials which might cause interference with other people would be used in small sound-proofed study rooms around the library. This would give a pattern of the kind shown in *Fig.* 104, possibly on two floors and interconnected by a lift.

191

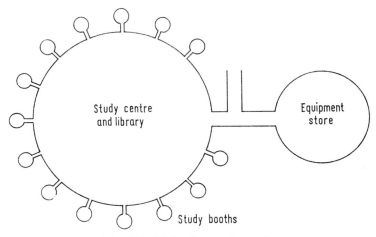

FIG. 104. Basis of a learning centre

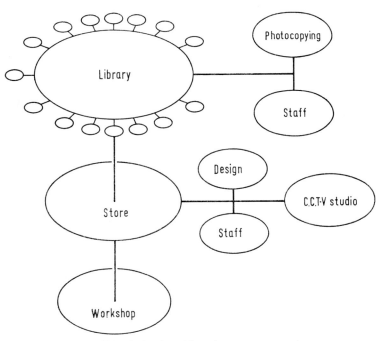

FIG. 105. A developed learning-resources centre

192

Since equipment must be maintained in first-class working condition a workshop should be provided for the technician staff within easy reach of the centre. Television services would also make major demands upon both the technical staff and the resources centre and consequently the studio would also be situated within this area (*Fig.* 105). Putting together in block

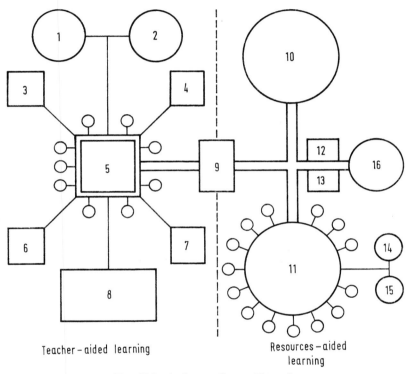

Teacher–aided learning

Resources–aided learning

FIG. 106. A place to live and learn in

1. Common rooms and recreation area
2. Dining cafeteria area
3. Sciences
4. Technologies
5. Staff workrooms and tutorial rooms
6. Liberal and general studies
7. Crafts
8. Physical education

9. Administration and staff common room for all staff
10. Equipment stores
11. Library with study rooms (carols)
12. Workshop and maintenance area
13. Design area
14. Photo-copying and microfilming
15. Staff workroom
16. C.C.T.V. Studio

schematic form the learning needs which have been discussed might result in the arrangement shown in *Fig.* 106.

STAFFING

Such a concentration of learning sources and facilities calls not only for a professional and technical staff but also for clerical assistants able to produce handouts, cope with inquiries and support the specialist staff, and for a graphics assistant able to produce illustrations and generally advise on aesthetic matters. The staff of this area for a college of 1,000 students might be as shown in *Fig.* 107.

Classrooms and laboratories would be grouped for organizational convenience but both their physical sizes and their use should be flexible. For

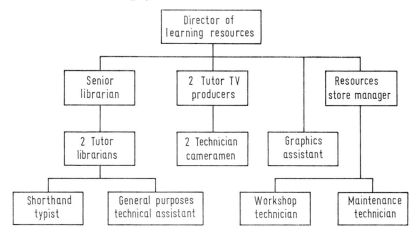

FIG. 107. Staff of a learning resources centre for a college of one thousand students

example, the laboratories might be designed to an open plan so that students could learn *science* and not physics in one closed room, biology in another and chemistry in a third.

The preparation room could be in a central position with the materials separated into subject groupings for convenience and there could, with profit,

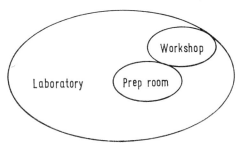

FIG. 108. First stage in laboratory planning

be a workshop for making equipment, within the laboratory area (*Fig.* 108).

Services can be carried along ducts in the walls and laboratory tables arranged to suit the varying needs of practical work. For example, at intervals of six feet around the walls, there might be groups of outlets for electricity, water and gas, so situated that laboratory tables could be serviced when

194

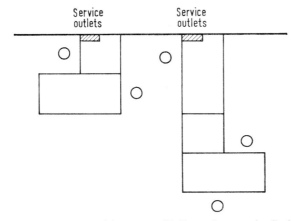

FIG. 109. Tables in a laboratory. Uniform sizes restrict flexibility

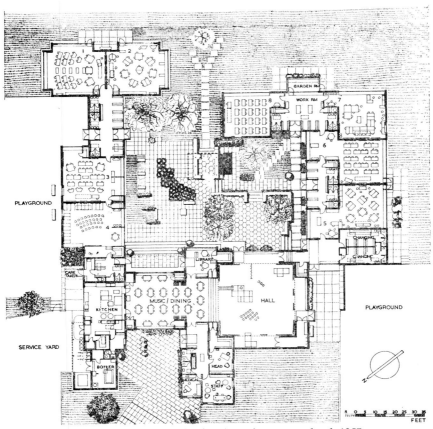

FIG. 110. Primary School at Amersham: completed, 1957

(*Reproduced by permission of the Department of Education and Science*)

195

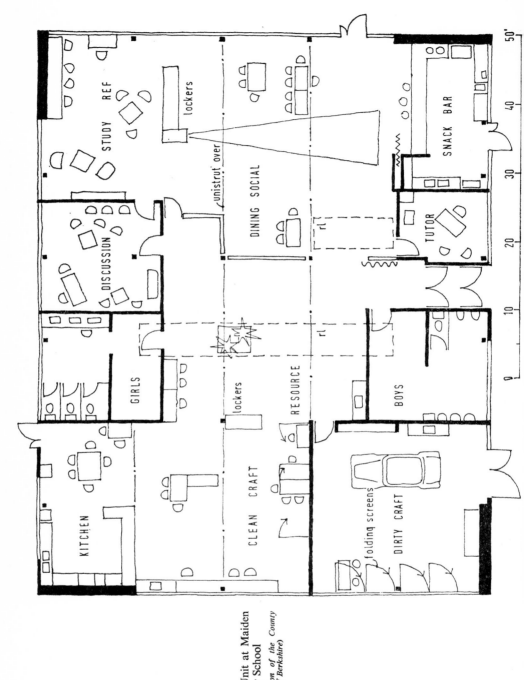

FIG. 111. Fifth Form Unit at Maiden Erleigh Secondary School

(Reproduced by kind permission of the County Architect of the Royal County of Berkshire)

placed alongside them. Open ring mains are invaluable for connecting anything to anything from anywhere to anywhere and are most useful if they
consist of a ring for each one or two rooms with linking points between them.
The tables themselves can be designed to make a variety of configurations

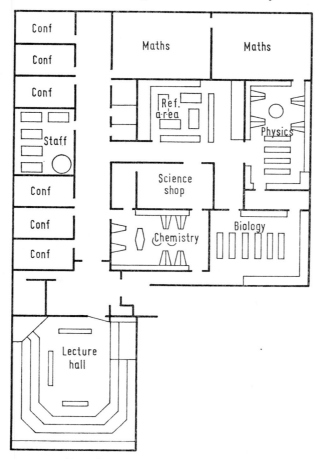

FIG. 112. Science Unit at Waylands School, U.S.A.

(*Fig.* 109). The enormously heavy laboratory tables which are common have
very few merits and do not lend themselves to adaptability.

A similar flexibility should characterize the planning of all parts of schools
and colleges. This would enable the needs of the learners to be as closely
matched by their environment as is possible. It also permits different shapes,
sizes and arrangements of groupings to suit discussion work, practical work,
individual work, film viewing and so on. *Fig.* 110 shows the plan of a Primary
School at Amersham designed by the Department of Education Development

197

Group[1] with these aims in mind, whilst *Fig.* 111 shows a fifth form unit designed for Maiden Erleigh Secondary School, Berkshire. The illustrations on the end papers show a plan of the Sixth-Form Centre at Rosebery County School for Girls at Epsom in Surrey.[2] The ground floor includes a lecture theatre to accommodate up to 112 girls, a make-up room with facilities appropriate for young adults, and also a large partially subdivided open common room area designed to satisfy a wide range of individual and group

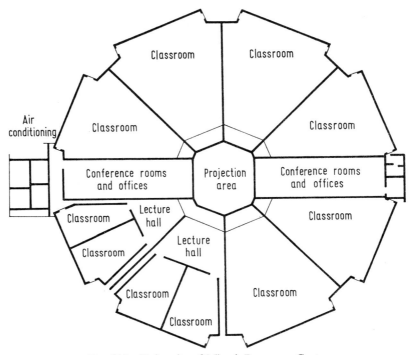

FIG. 113. University of Miami, Resources Centre

needs. This last area is carpeted, to reduce noise, as are several other areas in the building (see First Floor Plan).

On the first floor there is provision for three primary types of activity—the seminar, the tutorial and private study. These are grouped so that some of each type, in combination, can become the base for a particular subject or group of subjects. The unit contains 110 carols[3] (for 300 girls) each wired for lighting and for a variety of electrically driven teaching aids including tape recorders. See Plates 7 and 8.

Fig. 112 is an illustration of an American science unit at Waylands. *Fig.* 113 is the resources centre at the University of Miami.

198

INDUSTRIAL TRAINING

Industrial training rooms too, are being planned for greater flexibility and *Fig.* 114 shows a training room which is suitable for a variety of needs.

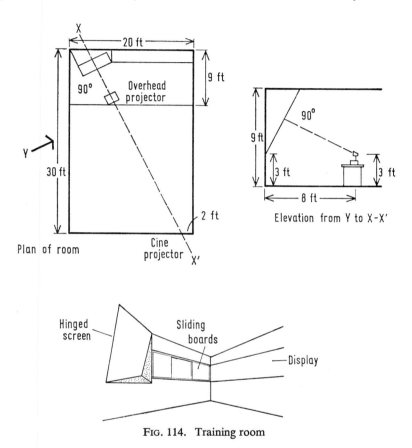

FIG. 114. Training room

The BACIE training room at Regent's Terrace, is based upon a very similar design (Plate 5).

The room can quickly be:
1. Cleared of furniture and used for informal meetings.
2. Furnished formally with chairs for lectures, film viewing or informally for relaxation, informal discussion or refreshments.
3. Furnished formally with chairs and tables for instructional meetings or informally for individual study or practical work.
4. Divided to provide seminar, syndicate, tutorial or interviewing rooms.

199

It is fitted for television viewing, closed circuit television, film viewing and overhead projection.

If it is inconvenient to bring trainees in to a central training establishment then the trainers might go to the trainees. This, the Southern Gas Board does using a fully equipped vehicle manned by specially trained staff (see Plate 6).

LARGE LECTURE THEATRES

A last example is chosen to illustrate the kinds of contributions which educationists should make towards the planning of a large and expensive lecture theatre. The basic problems which must be met in such a project stem from human needs, not, as so often seems to be implied, from purely aesthetic, purely economic or purely prestige pressures. The lecturer, for example, must be able to see his students, hear himself speak, conduct and control demonstrations and control the visual presentation: the students must be comfortable—and this means more than upholstered seats; it means seats in which it is possible to change position and even take up somewhat ungainly positions—be able to see and hear and feel their attention to be drawn towards the lecturer and his illustrations.

In the planning stage these needs reduce to technical problems of building construction, ergonomics, heating, ventilation, acoustics, illumination and so on and since they frequently make conflicting demands their relative weightings must be determined co-operatively by technical experts and educationists— the latter gathering ideas from colleagues, students, technicians, catering, clerical and maintenance staffs.

Certain characteristics of a lecture theatre are more or less fixed before the planning begins: they may vary within a little from time to time or place to place but they are available to all as building regulations or as research findings. There should, for instance, be about eighty cubic feet of space per person in order to provide sufficient air for breathing comfortably and the area to be occupied by each seated person should be about seven and a half square feet. For comfortable viewing* the distance from the screen to the viewer should lie between $2w$ and $6w$ where w is the width of the screen and no lines of vision should make an angle of more than about 30° with the normal to the centre of the screen: the bottom edge of the screen should be higher than the top of the lecturer's head. Unless a hall is built without regard to cost, these measurements impose limits on the shape. *Fig.* 115 (*top*) shows one set of limits in a plan view whilst *Fig.* 115 (*bottom*) shows another in a vertical section.

But space and viewing angles are the two most evident parameters which too often dominate design to the detriment of acoustics, ventilation and sound

* See page 121.

insulation. And although speech reinforcement equipment can make it possible to hear an otherwise inaudible lecturer it can never make an acoustically bad lecture room into an acoustically good one. The acoustical standards

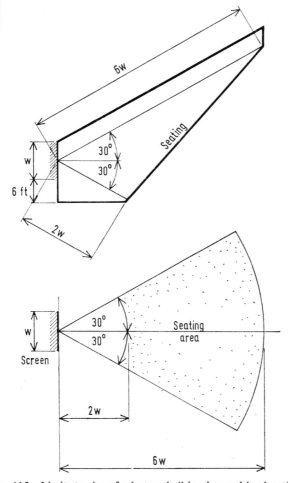

FIG. 115. Limits to size of a lecture hall in plan and in elevation

should therefore be planned so that, for example, the path length of reflected sound should not exceed that of the direct sound reaching any listener by more than sixty feet in order to avoid echo effects, so that the absorptions by empty seats should be roughly the same as that of students sitting in them and so on. Room sections for good acoustics are similar to those for good viewing conditions. A straight rear wall is often used to reduce focusing of reflected sound (*Fig.* 116) and a low broken ceiling profile provides differential indirect reinforcement to even out the total sound reaching each listener within five milliseconds of leaving the source (*Fig.* 117).

An acoustically well designed lecture theatre to hold 400 students should

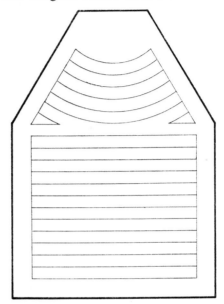

FIG. 116. Plan for satisfactory acoustics

need no speech reinforcement system provided there is no interference from external noise. Psychologically, amplified speech tends to dehumanize the lecturer and make him more remote: in the limit, his moving lips and gestures

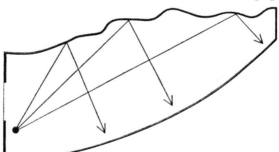

FIG. 117. Section for satisfactory acoustics

appear to keep time with what he is saying rather than to be the cause of what is heard. Also, since the acoustical feedback to the lecturer must be kept below the level at which the microphones re-amplify the loudspeaker output and cause "singing", the lecturer himself does not fully sense the sound for which he is responsible. This weakens the lecturer's ability to colour and

202

shape his communication so as to accommodate his ideas and consequently, both the lecturer and his audience become more conscious of the one-way nature of the process.

For larger theatres amplification systems are essential and these should be of the highest quality. The loudspeakers should be so positioned as to

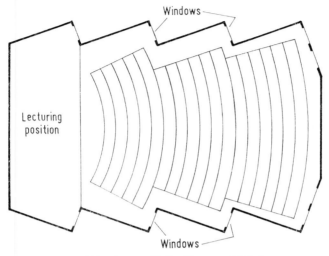

FIG. 118.   Lecture Hall with natural lighting

give the impression that the sound is coming from the speaker (or the screen) and the amplification should be adjustable from the seating area.

Lighting should be sufficient for note taking and dimming necessary only for the showing of colour films or transparencies in which colour is critical. Natural lighting is unsatisfactory because it varies considerably and windows, in any case, make sound insulation difficult and temperature control more costly. The absence of natural lighting creates no problems. There should, of course, be full air conditioning. If it is necessary to have windows they should not be in the line of view of the audience (*Fig.* 118). In this case, back projection arrangements are desirable.

Beyond a certain size of lecture theatre, the apparent dissociation of the lecturer from what he is saying becomes greater than it would if closed circuit television were used. Then, a saving in capital cost together with an improvement in group arrangement might be effected by using a semicircular seating arrangement with steeply tiered seats. Here the lecturer would use a television writing and display surface (which is like an overhead projector writing surface) and telecine for films: there would be no screens or boards (*Fig.* 119).

The cost of building a lecture room theatre is a high capital investment from which a high return in educational activity should be expected. Although they are frequently built to serve for lectures *and* dramatic productions or

203

dining rooms, architects and building engineers are generally agreed that such rooms cannot efficiently be designed to fulfil more than one function and consequently should be capable of very frequent use. This is often difficult

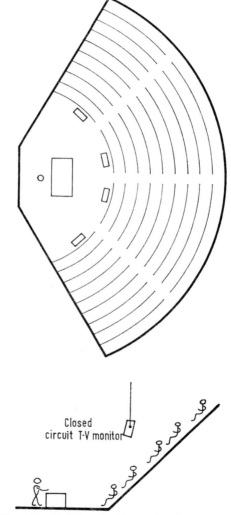

Closed
circuit T-V monitor

FIG. 119. Hall for television-assisted presentations

because of the time needed for the preparation of demonstrations and the setting up of equipment, and consequently a way must be found of preparing the hall for one lecture whilst it is still in use for another.

This can be solved by using a revolving stage on which are three separate sections each fully equipped with writing surfaces, screen, lecturing bench and so on. Whilst the first lecture of the day is in progress, the next two will be in course of preparation in the adjacent preparation rooms. When the first lecture ends, the stage is rotated and any final touches completed in a few minutes.

The materials and equipment used in the first lecture are now dismantled and returned to store and the third lecture setting prepared in readiness for the next change-over. In this way the hall can be fully utilized.

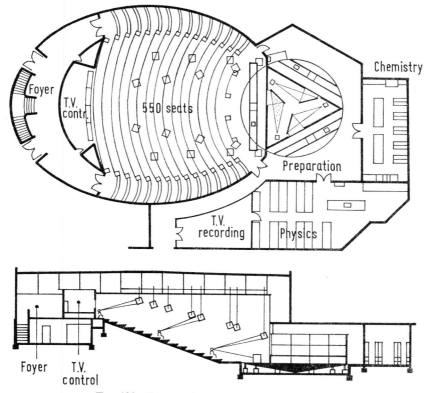

Fig. 120. Lecture theatre at Berkeley, California

Naturally, all the possible reasonable lecturing requirements should be built into the structure. Television monitors should be suspended from the ceiling so that small scale demonstrations can be viewed in comfort, the hall itself should be acoustically unimpeachable and unobtrusively fitted with microphones and amplifiers for speech reinforcement. These ideas find expression in the lecture theatre at Berkeley, California shown in *Fig.* 120.[4]

The difficulty of moving teaching equipment from one place to another will remain, however good the planning, and this constitutes a problem of no small magnitude. Small service lifts should be fitted at convenient points in

15—(T.1164)

the building and instead of the familiar tea-trolley, smaller electrically-driven lift trucks have become, very nearly, a necessity. These would make it a simple matter to raise large numbers of books to top shelves, to transfer machines and materials safely and quietly, and to remove the criticism which technicians quite reasonably make when they are employed as porters to move unwieldy loads.

Lecture theatres must, of course, be designed by experts, but the implications of designs must be appreciated in advance by teachers. Almost all of the large lecture theatres in colleges of education and technical colleges are bad lecture theatres (bad dining rooms, bad cinemas, bad theatres and bad dance halls) simply because they have been thought of only from the point of view of cost, volume, area and fire regulations and not from the point of view of the efficient communication of ideas.

It is not the purpose of this work to attempt to offer solutions to planning problems, since this is the combined function of architects, engineers and teachers. This brief outline shows glimpses of some ways in which new media present new opportunities in planning and it will have served its purpose if it has drawn attention to the kind of thinking which should lead to the final plan—certainly the plan of a machine to learn in, but also a machine to serve learners, prepared by people who believe learning to be an essential component of living happy, purposeful and co-operative lives.

And this is it. We began by considering the most important aspects of learning theory and then used them to develop communications strategies for teaching small groups on the one hand and large groups on the other. We then reviewed the devices which can be used in teaching and the modifications which their use imposes upon planning and upon the roles of staff. Finally we looked at these new groupings of things and their requirements, and people and their needs, and wrapped walls around them to contain them in proper envelopes.

And it ends as it began. Teaching is communication. When we have dusted away all the jargon about the processes which go on inside machines we are left with the fact—becoming almost a surprising fact—that only *living things* communicate. Machines and devices are there to extend our opportunities for giving professional service; to ask more of them is to abdicate our responsibilities.

REFERENCES

1. MINISTRY OF EDUCATION, *Building Bulletin No.* 16. August 1958. Development Projects: Junior School, Amersham.
2. MINISTRY OF EDUCATION, *Building Bulletin* 41, Sixth-Form Centre, HMSO, 1967, 59 pp.
3. MINISTRY OF EDUCATION, *Building Bulletin* 25, Secondary School Design; Sixth-Form and Staff, HMSO, 1965.

4. HARVEY E. WHITE, New Physical Sciences Lecture Hall, *American Journal of Physics*, Vol. 33, No. 12, Dec. 1965. (Describes the hall of the Berkeley Campus of the University of California.)

FURTHER READING

DUNCAN, C. J. (Ed.) *Modern Lecture Theatres*, Manchester, Oriel Press Ltd., 1966.
TAYLOR, J., *The Science Lecture Room—a planning study*, 119 pp., Cambridge University Press, 1967.

APPENDIX 1: Basic equipment for a resources centre

The equipment suggested here is for a college of 1,000 full-time students or the equivalent. Naturally since needs, interests and conditions vary, this list is not to be taken as a blueprint but as a starting point for planning.

1   16-mm cine projector with a 1-kW lamp, a 2-in. lens, a 6-in. × 4-in. internal speaker and a good separate speaker (a 12-in. speaker or a 4-unit line source), with a 50-ft lead, an output of about 15 watts and magnetic/optical, record/replay facilities.

1   16-mm cine projector as above but without magnetic record/replay facilities.
(Check the focal length of the lens required. For back projection a 1-in. lens will probably be needed.)

1   8-mm super-8, 150 W lamp, silent film projector.

1   8-mm super-8, 150 W, sound film projector.

1   dual-gauge standard/super-8, 150 W, silent film projector.

4   super-8 silent cassette-loading film loop projectors.

12   overhead projectors.

2   filmstrip projectors with remote control.

4   automatic slide projectors with 150 W quartz-iodine lamps and with remote control.

1   episcope with 10 in. × 10 in. and 1,000-W lamp.

1   microprojector.

4   projector stands which are easy to move, can be locked into position and adjusted for level. Folding stands should be chosen only if this facility is very desirable.

1   high quality 2-track stereophonic tape recorder with speeds $7\frac{1}{2}$, $3\frac{3}{4}$ and $1\frac{7}{8}$ in. per second.

3   good 2-track reasonably portable tape recorders.

3   small cartridge-loading battery portable tape recorders.

2   slide synchronizers for use with the tape recorders.
Spare microphones.

2   record playing decks.

2 amplifiers with inputs for record, radio, tape and microphone, 10-W output.
3 suitably enclosed loudspeakers.
1 radio receiver—battery portable.
2 portable television receivers with 23-in. screens.
1 8-mm film camera for super-8 film with reflex viewfinder and automatic exposure.
1 robust tripod with pan and tilt head.
4 lights: 3 soft (fillers) and 1 spot.
2 television cameras with built-in electronic viewfinders.
1 television camera for captions.
2 rolling tripods with pan and tilt heads.
1 vision mixer.
1 sound mixer.
4 8-in. monitors.
1 video-tape recorder.
3 television monitors with 23-in. screens.
8 lights: 6 soft (fillers) and 2 spots, cabling, etc. for television equipment.
2 portable rear-projection screens, say about 3 ft wide.
2 portable tilting screens, say about 5 ft square.
1 box screen, say, about 8 ft square.
2 spirit duplicators (others will be departmentally owned).
1 flat-bed thermal copier suitable for making transparencies.
1 film splicer for 8-mm film (super).
1 film rewinder for 16-mm and 8-mm film (super) with spare spools.
1 film viewer for editing.
1 35-mm camera.
1 tripod.
1 photographic enlarger and all accessories.
1 copying stand.
1 tape splicer.
1 tape editor.

Teaching machines as required and if not departmentally owned.

TOOLS FOR PREPARING AIDS

Small power drilling machine and set of drills
Small metal turning lathe and tools
Steel rule
Steel square
Razor-type knife
Steel plane

Cross-cut saw
Dovetail saw
Fret-saw
Mitre box
Cutting board
Small hammer
Medium hammer
Marking knife
Wood chisels
Files—medium and small
Shears for tinplate
Guillotine for card
Scissors
Screwdrivers
Centre punch
Small spanners
Pincers
Pliers
Mallet
Bradawl
Wood vice
Metal vice
Soldering bit
Solder, flux, nails, screws, glue
Glass paper and emery cloth

MATERIALS FOR PREPARING AIDS

Newsprint: double-crown size
Paper, cartridge—30 in. × 22 in.
Card, Manila, 100 lb, double-crown size
Card, mounting, 40 in. × 40 in., black, grey, and white
Pencils
Drawing boards and T-squares
Rules, squares and compasses
Mapping pens
Felt-tipped pens—assorted colours
Penholders and script nibs
Mars Omnichrom pencils or similar
Mars Technical fountain pen or similar
Masking tape
Wax crayons—large
Brush, decorator's
Brushes, sable

Indian ink
White ink
Poster paints—assorted
Powder colours—assorted
Coloured etching inks for writing on acetate (Pelikan Type K)
Coloured inks for writing on acetate (Pelikan Type T)
Spirit ink remover
Dry transfer lettering
Self-adhesive transparent coloured film and tape
Adhesives including paste, latex-based and resin-based adhesives
Bostik 252 adhesive
Sellotape
Felt, best quality, black, to cover area about 3 ft × 4 ft for felt board
Felt squares in assorted colours
Lint, white or gridded flock paper
Acetate roll for overhead projector
Acetate sheets (10 in. × 10 in.)
Polythene sheets (10 in. × 10 in.)
Card frames (aperture 10 in. × 10 in.)
Perspex offcuts
Perspex cement
Wood—in variety
Hardboard offcuts
Tinplate, medium thickness (30 gauge)
Magnets—disc
Magnetic plastic strip, plastic sheet and string
Splicing cement
Splicing tape
Stapler and staples

APPENDIX 2: Examples of objective type tests

1. Complete the following sentences:

(a) Gas pressure may be measured with a water ....

(b) A ball rolling from rest down a frictionless slope travels 1 ft in the first second. It will travel .... ft in the first two seconds.

(c) The coefficient of cubical expansion is..................times the coefficient of linear expansion of the same material.

(d) 3 miles + 4 miles = ...: 3 miles due N + 4 miles due E = ... (omit the direction).

(e) The reaction at a smooth surface always acts........................

(f) Kinetic energy = $\frac{1}{2}m$............. It is measured in............ in the SI system.

(g) The centre of gravity of a body is the point at which........................

(h) If a gas expands whilst its pressure remains constant, its temperature ....

(i) Pressure is........................

(j) The mechanical equivalent of heat is about............joules/calorie.

(k) The triangle of forces law refers to three forces acting.................... in equilibrium.

(l) Convection currents in water, due to heating its surface, will flow only between the temperatures of..............°C and ....°C.

(m) The sum of the vectors represented by a.................figure is zero.

2. Cross out the one or two incorrect alternatives in each group below.

(a) The product of a force and a distance may give
work done
torque
power

(b) Two iron weights, one ten times as heavy as the other, fall the same height to the ground. The temperature of the heavy one will rise about

the same amount
ten times as much as that of the light one
a tenth as much

Displacement
(c) Acceleration is given by the area under a velocity–time graph.
Force

                      heat per unit of work
(d) The mechanical equivalent of heat is the work per unit of heat
                            number of joules/calorie

Kinetic energy
(e) Force   is equal to rate of change of momentum.
Time

                  radians/second
(f) Angular velocity may be measured in degrees/minute
                      revolutions
(g) The reaction to a force acting on a smooth plane surface will be
    along the plane
    perpendicular to the plane
    at any angle to the plane

3. Each item in the list on the left is equal to an item in the list on the right. Decide which, and write its letter in the space provided.

(a) Angular velocity of 8 rad/s	30 hp	....
(b) Joule's equivalent × heat produced	zero	....
(c) Rate of change of momentum	m/s	....
(d) SI unit of velocity	force	....
(e) Pressure 10 ft below water surface	20 hp	....
(f) Density of substance/s.g.	625 lb/ft²	....
(g) Coefficient of expansion of iron	work done	....
(h) Sum of three forces in equilibrium	load	....
(i) 16,500 ft-lbf/s	density of water	....
(j) 14,920 watts	240 rev/min	....
(k) Effort × M.A.	0·000012/degC	....

214

INDEX

215

PLATES

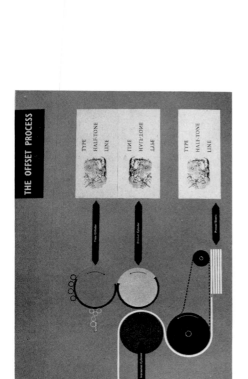

(T.1164)

PLATE 1.

(*Top*) Examples of teaching charts produced by teachers of printing during their professional training for teaching at Garnett College. Notice the economy of subject detail, the absence of written explanations and the implied concern for elegant layout

(*Bottom left*) Charts for display produced by teachers of printing whilst training at Garnett College. Notice here the appeal of the three-dimensional arrangement and the "problem" which challenges the viewers: where to start and which way to follow around the stand. Notice too the relatively full explanation

PLATE 2.

(*Top*) Loop film projector with a back projection screen
  (*Courtesy Technicolor Ltd.*)

(*Bottom left*) Loop film projector built into back projection screen
  (*Courtesy Rank Audio Visual Ltd.*)

(*Bottom right*) Loop film projector built into back projection screen
  (*Courtesy ICEM Ltd.*)

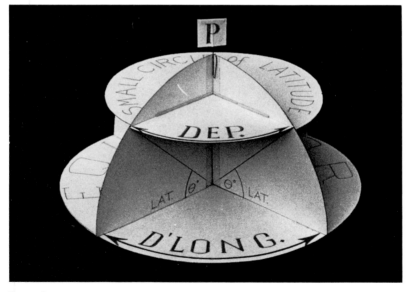

PLATE 3.

(*Top*) Components of a cardboard model for students who are learning navigation.
Made by D. W. P. Varwell, photograph by C. Bird

(*Bottom*) The model assembled. Notice its simplicity. A student who finds difficulty
in following the mathematics when it is supported by a two-dimensional diagram
can refer to the model for more realistic information. Photograph by C. Bird

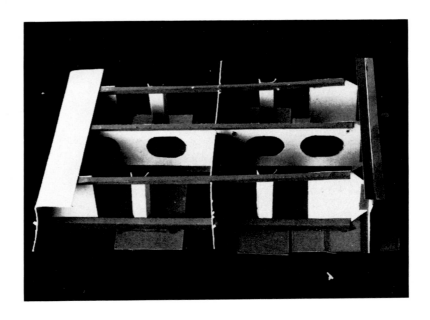

PLATE 4.

(*Top*) Cardboard model illustrating an aspect of ship construction made by a teacher of nautical subjects whilst training at Garnett College. Photograph by C. Bird.

(*Bottom*) A more complex model also made from card. This is a contour model painted on its surface to show geological outcrops and along its side to show geological sections. Photograph by C. Bird

PLATE 5.

(*Top*) Training sales staff using closed circuit television at the Southern Gas Board's Training Centre

(*Bottom*) The training room at BACIE

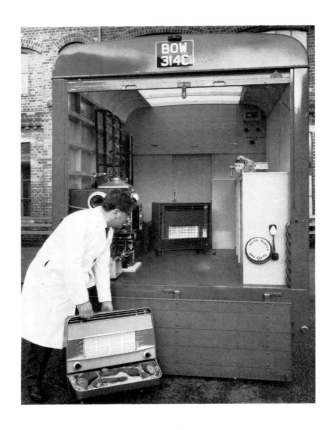

PLATE 6.

Fully equipped vehicles for on-site training
(*Reproduced by kind permission of the Chief Education and Training Officer,
Southern Gas Board*)

PLATE 7.

Sixth Form Centre at Rosebery County School, Epsom

(*Plates 7 and 8 reproduced by kind permission of the Department of Education and Science*)

(*Top*) One of the open suites which provide accommodation for either a seminar or for a tutorial and private study or for just private study

(*Bottom*) The large group room on the first floor which is used for discussions, listening to music, etc.

PLATE 8.

(*Left*) A group of carols
(*Right*) The snack-bar area